JOHN BROOKES
Garden Masterclass

JOHN BROOKES

Garden Masterclass

A DORLING KINDERSLEY BOOK

London, New York, Melbourne, Munich, Delhi

Produced for Dorling Kindersley by Walton and Pringle
www.waltonandpringle.com
Art Editor Colin Walton

Senior Managing Editor Anna Kruger
Senior Managing Art Editor Lee Griffiths

DTP Louise Waller
Production Controller Heather Hughes

Illustrations Richard Lee
Picture Research Melanie Watson

First published in Great Britain in 2002
by Dorling Kindersley Limited, 80 Strand, London WC2R 0RL. A Penguin Company
Copyright © 2002 Dorling Kindersley Limited. Text copyright © 2002 John Brookes

2 4 6 8 10 9 7 5 3 1

A Cataloging-in-Publication record for this title is available from the Library of Congress
ISBN 0-7894-8382-3

Colour reproduction by GRB Editrice, s.r.l., Verona, Italy; cover and jacket by Colourscan,
Singapore
Printed and bound by A Mondadori Editore, Verona, Italy

See our complete catalog at
www.dk.com

contents

foreword

In my Masterclass, I want to explain the way I think about garden design, explaining the logical process behind what can, after all, be an ephemeral art form.

First I have to make it clear that it is the art of design that interests me primarily, not the craft of horticulture. I seem to have spent half a lifetime trying to explain the difference, and my preference, to a public and a clientele who are often deeply horticultural – in my native Britain anyway.

Many people, I find, have little feeling for design, though they might be hugely sensitive to nature, and for some, design is almost an embarrassing word. For the young, design has had more to do with labels on clothes, cars, or kitchens, and seldom for anything outdoors. But now garden design has become the intended profession of more students than ever before, and more British garden owners, confronted with an excess of television makeovers, profess a requirement for good design. I believe more passionately than ever that we need good design and to know where it comes from, so join me on a journey through some of my twentieth-century landscape experiences. Historically, it has been an amazing time for all of us; things have moved and changed so fast – this then is a garden designer's response to it.

It has taken a long time to come about, but finally we are beginning to think of the garden in its setting. This setting is not just to do with the physical, and we need to realize that we are as much part of an environment as the plants and wildlife growing in it. We are all beginning to recognize that the spirit of the place in which we live is both unique and fragile.

Environmental concern has always tended to be someone else's problem, but the issue is relevant to each and every one of us – any storm, or even a high wind, let alone a flood or an earthquake, demonstrates all too clearly how we, our houses and gardens, are subject to environmental happenings.

All these facets of our lives bring the conservation issue into the garden of every householder and, I suspect, nearly every reader of this book.

The preservation of our landscapes, of which your garden is part, is vital – and to do this we have to discover the essence of our own particular place and work with it. Garden design is my concern, but its continuing relationship with nature is my desire.

John Brookes

introduction

Discoveries and influences formulate your ideas. It is only in retrospect that one realizes how true this is. This is my own "voyage of discovery" in garden design.

Like most people, the starting point in my experience of gardens was the secure, linear, suburban garden. Indeed as a child I probably could not have imagined any other kind of garden, for one was brought up to obey conventions and to appreciate "law and order" – and that meant a path straight down the middle. Things could happen on either side – but some sort of balance was essential. The suburban garden was a metaphor for life.

It never occurred to me or my family that new art forms or ideas could influence our thoughts on this. Modernism wasn't even considered, beyond perhaps a chuckle at a flat roof despite the fact that one of my grandfathers had been an architect. My father's side of the family were all civil engineers with feet firmly placed upon very practical ground.

But I did have a feeling for space. This may have come from my school connection with Durham Cathedral and long services one could scarcely hear and often not even see – so far away was the action. But the soaring roof and monumental supporting Norman columns are still memorable.

I also have a very clear memory of being "ribbed" by my brother for loving the entrance foyer of a local cinema. It was very late 1930s, all chrome and marble with curving corners and upturned light fixtures. I realize now that this was a crude, popularized version of Modernism – but to me it was exhilarating.

I experienced nothing of grand formality in gardens until much later in my life. Any minor country houses we visited were landscaped in the park style or were planted with vegetables in the 1940s and 1950s.

Later, during my apprenticeship with Nottingham Parks Department, I visited Melbourne Hall in Derbyshire, one of those formal gardens in the French style, which may have been influenced by Le Nôtre, the seventeenth-century French garden designer. And then, when I was a landscape student at University College, London, we visited St. Paul's Waldenbury, a formal garden praised by the landscape architect Geoffrey Jellicoe. Athough I didn't realize it at the time, I was learning about what remained of the formal tradition in Britain – and in that

an early influence

I went to school in Durham City, and every day for 12 years or so I saw, and often was at a service, in the cathedral. Our school boathouse was just to the right of the weir, and I rowed on the great loop of the river running around this amazing Norman building most afternoons in my later school years. This beautiful tranquil setting of trees running down to the river was, I am sure, an enormous influence on my perception of how to shape the landscape.

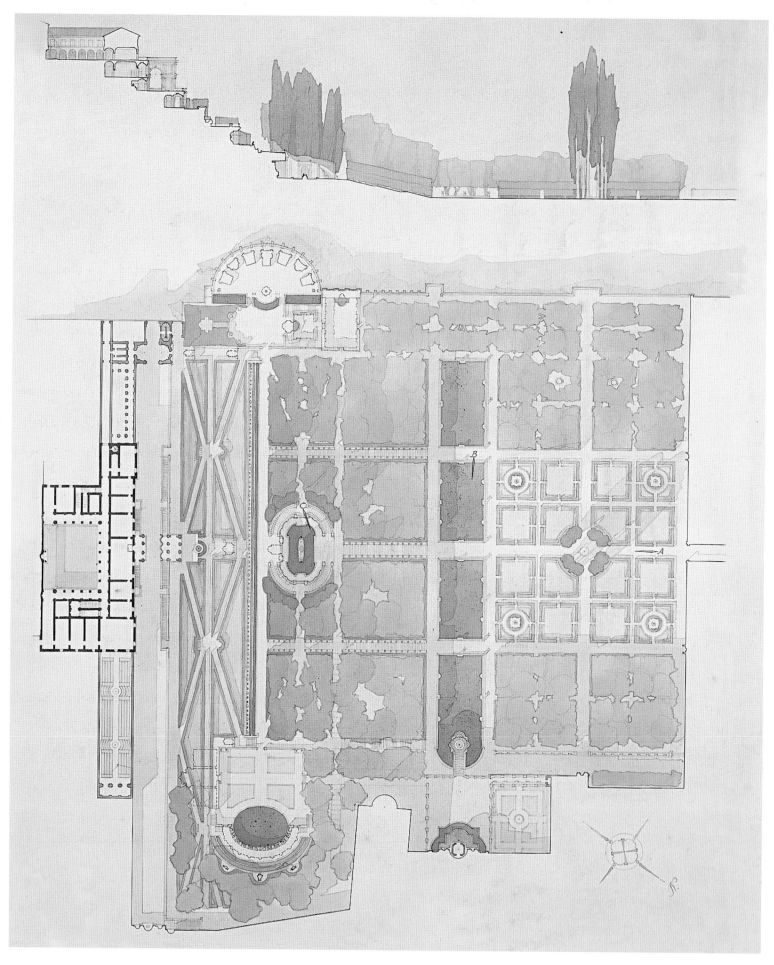

"I took day trips to Tivoli, to d'Este and to the Villa Ariane, and the light began to dawn. I was starting to understand."

particular garden a feeling for the linear structure of avenues of trees punctuated by open-hedged rooms. This was garden design on a grand scale.

Later, staying at the British School in Rome, I started to explore Italian gardens. Again Geoffrey Jellicoe was my guide, specifically his book *The Gardens of Italy*, co-written with J.C. Shepherd. The drawings were superb and a great help in appreciating the layout of the gardens I visited. I must truthfully confess that after a number of years at a good school I still had only a vague idea what the Renaissance was about. This first visit was an eye-opener. I belonged to the war generation that didn't want to know about Europe. My father had been wounded in World War I in France. To that narrow mindset, anything foreign was taboo. But if one reflects a moment on the misery of the trenches in which he was wounded it is, I suppose, very understandable.

So on my first Italian trip I was finding my way. Italy was a revelation – all I had previously known of it came from the faded pages of a dull Latin primer and the pompous prose of Sir George Sitwell's *On the Making of Gardens*. Now for myself I found it alive and vibrant. (Many years later, I stayed at Renishaw in Derbyshire, Sir George's home and garden – and then I appreciated what he was about!) At that time, too, people traveled to Italy by train, with the excitement of waking up to the beauty of the Alps, then the Po valley, then the spires and buttresses of Milan cathedral, and so on, until the final revelation of Rome itself. Being alone, I was pretty terrified, but totally exhilarated.

I walked Rome, its gardens and hidden corners. I took day trips to Tivoli, to d'Este, and to the Villa Ariane, and the light began to dawn. I was starting to understand. (Georgina Masson's book *Italian Gardens* subsequently explained a lot more about the formal layout in the Renaissance garden.)

On a later visit, I discovered the Villa Marlia outside beautiful Lucca in northern Italy. This was a garden that had been owned by Napoleon's sister. Although surrounded by a park in

formal Italian ideas

TOP Italian gardens had little to do with horticulture, and everything to do with theater, coolness, the play of light and dark, and the sound of splashing water. These gardens were as sculpted in their spatial layouts as the buildings from which they developed. Time has softened the effect of this layout of intricate geometry.
LEFT A plan and section of the Villa d'Este garden from the Jellicoe and Shepherd book *Gardens of Italy*. I enjoyed the gently rendered technique of the drawings.

"I was beginning to discover that formal was not necessarily linear – asymmetry could be as formal as symmetry."

the English style, the small remaining formal Renaissance garden was very beautiful. The pearl of it was a square balustraded pond, surrounded by evergreens. Sailing on the pond were a family of swans, which brought the whole thing to life. This tranquility is what many of the great formal gardens lack – crowds of tourists do not bring about the same effect!

After Italian Renaissance gardens I needed to discover French ones. My first ventures to France had been the South, with friends, on beach vacations in my late teens. At that time it was still fairly novel to be there, though one heard that Winston Churchill stayed quite near by. One of the gardens I visited was Les Colombières at Menton, very dilapidated but still retaining huge romantic charm. I had read about mood in a garden, and this was the first time I had experienced it. The garden is now being restored. It has formal elements in it, but also a sense of 1930s modernity, the work of Ferdinand Bac. This was the first time I witnessed a sense of French modern style, too, or as Bac called it, "Mediterranean."

Years later with students I visited the restored garden of the Vicomte de Noailles at Hyères, designed by Guevrékian – a Cubist garden design layout first shown at the Paris Decorative Arts exhibition in 1926.

I was beginning to discover that formal was not necessarily linear – asymmetry could be as formal as symmetry.

Driving north from one of these Mediterranean trips we visited Vaux le Vicomte and Versailles. I could feel the attraction of grand formal layouts, but I felt too that somehow the grand plan trapped the visitor. I never enjoyed that. The scale of those gardens is overwhelming. Later, on the East Coast of the U.S., I visited many grand nineteenth-century French-style gardens, which are also impressive in scale: Dumbarton Oaks in Washington D.C. in particular. Perhaps the style you favor is to do with temperament. The southern version of formal, which I preferred, was more comprehensible and relaxed. Quite often though, "this relaxed" appearance is, I have to acknowledge, a lack of rigorous maintenance – an example of faded elegance.

French influences

TOP Northern French geometry by Le Nôtre (1613-1700) in the garden of Vaux-le-Vicomte.
RIGHT On a trip to Menton during the 1960s, I discovered a small hotel set in a ravishingly moody and dilapidated garden called Les Colombières. Now under restoration, the garden seemed Classical to a degree, but contained what I would call "neo-Classical" decoration, the like of which I had never seen. It was designed by Ferdinand Bac, who lived there with the owners.

Later, when I ran summer schools for an American foundation at La Napoule near Cannes, I explored many smaller formal layouts throughout Provence, including at that time a rather run-down Serre de la Madone (designed by Lawrence Johnston, the creator of Hidcote), and some Russell Page gardens, too. The garden of the Château du Roy was memorable, with a Russell Page parterre. We also visited the Champins' garden at Le Chêvre d'Or outside Biot; and farther north, the small château garden of Gourdon, supposedly with Le Nôtre connections, though restored in 1919 by an American lady.

I can well understand why people attempt to achieve this relaxed formality time and again in stylish urban gardens in Britain, but it is never the same – you aren't on vacation for a start. Citrus are missing, and cypress do not grow, because of course the climate is different. No matter how much lavender you plant or oil jars you distribute, it never works properly, because you are being inspired by a southern style requiring a different light, impossible in a colder northern climate.

Nevertheless, the cliché of the small formal garden became a late-twentieth-century urban icon – often accompanied by uncomfortable metal chairs and a wobbling table!

But not all of it was bad. I remember a book by the designer David Hicks called *Garden Design* which impressed me – all still very grand in his own garden, although he was trying to scale it down in some of his book illustrations.

An important diversion in my exploration of the formal was a foray into the world of Islam. I never had understood the connection between the gardens of the south of Spain on one hand, and those of the Middle East and northern India on the other, and I determined to find out – seizing the opportunity when I moved to Tehran in the late 1970s to run a school of interior design. I had been in charge of the Inchbald School of Garden Design for some time (not a full-time post), and needed a break. Jacqueline Thwaites, the principal, said that she had been approached by the Iran Chamber of Commerce to run such a school and was I interested. To investigate the possibility, I took

classic elements

TOP The late David Hicks' own garden, The Grove, which interprets classic formality with a modern eye in an Oxfordshire landscape.
LEFT I had been overwhelmed by the plantsmanship of Lawrence Johnston at Hidcote in Gloucestershire, but in the South of France I talked my way into his romantic, overgrown garden at Serre de la Madone near Menton, which at that time was hauntingly beautiful from its years of neglect.

"The garden is used as a metaphor for the afterlife in the Koran, the Muslim holy book. The use of water is central to the form of the garden."

a tour of Iran to explore that beautiful country. But to understand its art, architecture, and gardens, I had to learn something about Islam. My guide was the Islamic expert, the late Anthony Hutt. He unlocked this door for me, and later we went to Moorish Spain, where my understanding deepened.

Islamic gardens are, of course, formal – indeed one of the more appealing things about the Islamic religion and way of life is its order. The term "garden" for a British person is perhaps misleading in this context because gardens in Iran are seldom floriferous. The garden is used as a metaphor for the afterlife in the Koran, the Muslim holy book. The use of water is central to the form of the garden. Water is a scarce commodity, and therefore a precious ingredient, and quite often pools appear in a cruciform shape, representing what are known as the Four Rivers of Life (of wine, of water, of milk, and of clarified honey). Later in the Mughal gardens in northern India and in Kashmir, I saw more great Muslim gardens, where water is used in even more ingenious ways, but always formally.

The architect Sir Edwin Lutyens knew about the Islamic use of water, and one sees that influence in his country house gardens time and again. Examples include the simple tanks of water at the Deanery and the rills at Hestercombe. So the formality of the Muslim garden was brought to the English country house. Of course, many of the owners Lutyens designed for at that time had experienced life in the Mideast as well.

The end of the country-house period of British gardens coincided with the emergence of a Modernist movement in continental Europe. Broadly a militant left-wing movement, though primarily concerned with design, it was out of sympathy with Nazism and Fascism, and many of its proponents moved in the 1930s to the U.S., where Modernism became known as the International Movement. In 1938 Christopher Tunnard published *Gardens in the Modern Landscape*, which reproduced in book form his previous series of articles in the *Architectural Review*. There was a second edition in 1948. Reading this I realized that Modernism in Britain had passed me by. From the

Islamic inspiration

TOP After 20 years' absence, I recently returned to this lovely restored nineteenth-century garden – the Bagh-e Shahzadeh at Mahan, sitting on its own in the Iranian desert, but only coming to life when it is fed by water from the surrounding mountains.
RIGHT At Hestercombe, in Somerset, in a garden created in 1906 by the architect Sir Edwin Lutyens and plantswoman Gertrude Jekyll, two central rills (canals) owe much, I believe, to Islamic influences.

"From the end of World War II garden design influences came from the U.S. and the new abstracted forms of design they contained were a revelation to me ..."

outdoor living

Years before seeing it the simple beauty of many of the gardens designed by the late Thomas Church in northern California left me thunderstruck. The abstracted shape of this swimming pool at his El Novillero garden, Sonoma County epitomizes his work. I saw abstracted forms realized in landscape with places for people to relax outside in summer before the advent of air-conditioning.

end of World War II garden design influences came from the U.S. and the new abstracted forms of design they contained were a revelation to me, as was the concept of outdoor living, whereby the garden became an extension of the home.

Now, for the first time one saw the terrace and the swimming pool, with the lawn and surrounding plantings being used asymmetrically and for domestic pleasure. The classic symmetrical approach to designing gardens had been abandoned.

At the Festival of Britain in 1951, new garden style was demonstrated for the first time by Peter Shepherd, Russell Page, and Maria Shepherd among others; and a newer, more architectural form of planting started to emerge. At Battersea Festival Gardens there was a huge carnival, which Russell Page had designed in a formal idiom – but lively and frivolous with it. And in an increasingly prosperous postWar Britain, we were starting to build a new stock of townhouses with smaller gardens, and these new contemporary American ideas began to be interpreted in a British setting.

We were starting to reinterpret formality as well. Used correctly, the trim effect the style achieves gives an ordered symmetry that many people appreciate. Throughout the second half of the twentieth century, Dutch garden designers have, I believe, produced more interesting layouts than the British, who still seem to associate formality – no matter how reduced its scale – with grand renaissance decoration.

One recent inspiring example of Formalism has been the work of the Wirtz, father-and-son team, in Belgium. Father Jacques and son Peter are producing iconoclastic formal designs which have shown me at last that formality need not be dull, and that it can embrace some softness in its planting.

Traditionally, when a garden design was commissioned, a formal layout was expected by the client. But most garden design has been romantic in approach, conjuring up English cottage gardens where design was not really considered – rather just an abundance of flowers, herbs, soft fruit, and other plant material.

open-style housing

TOP The wife of Walter Gropius, the architect of this building wrote: "The house is opened up to take in part of the surrounding area and extends beyond its enclosing walls; it reaches out with 'tentacles' of trellis, low walls, and planting designed to delineate the outdoor living space throughout the year."

"One recent inspiring example of formalism has been the work of the Wirtz, father-and-son team, in Belgium."

It is this dichotomy of style preference that has beset taste-makers throughout the twentieth century, while in the middle of it all, the new small urban garden started to make an appearance – its evolution had little to do with either the classic formal or the traditional cottage idiom!

I had been so busy seeking inspiration from abroad I had missed out on the late nineteenth-century Arts and Crafts movement, seen in the work of the architect Sir Edwin Lutyens, the plantswoman Gertrude Jekyll, and the cottage garden. I was probably too close to it in fact, and had always been seeking to escape what I perceived as the cozy safeness of it all. But I was aware of William Robinson, a plantsman and writer who sought to rid gardens of their nineteenth-century inheritance of the half-hardy annual and what became known as bedding out. Robinson suggested using fewer startling aliens, and distributing plants in a semi-natural way. Miss Jekyll picked this up and wrote further of native plants, their habitat, and the very natural way in which cottage gardens were planted – early conservation literature, in fact.

As gardens became smaller and more widespread, a change in horticultural thinking took place. The eighteenth-century concern for parkland design was superseded by a concern for the use of plants in the garden: first of all within a geometric, often Italianate design, but later within a Lutyens-type arrangement aligned with the house. Gertrude Jekyll and her planting in the cottage garden idiom helped to soften Robinson's approach. This style became fashionable again fifty years later in the early 1980s with the reissue of Jekyll's book on planting design. It took me years to realize that soft, cottage-type, romantic planting can perfectly well overlay a modern garden design. It was in fact the strength of many Lutyens' layouts that held Jekyll's plantings together.

I had no sooner gotten these concepts right in my head than there started to be fresh rumblings about "the garden in its setting." This was brought home to me as I started to design larger country gardens and then gardens abroad. As I get older, this regard for the nuances of a particular landscape increases.

planting design

TOP I enjoy the order of the contemporary gardens of Jacques and Peter Wirtz, contrasted with a soft underplanting of decorative plant material.
RIGHT Gertrude Jekyll's writing was some of the first on planting design – this is a wonderfully restored, textural grouping at Hestercombe in Somerset, which she designed in 1906. The late-autumn effect is strongly architectural as well, making a suitable foil to the conservatory designed by Sir Edwin Lutyens.

"I had been so busy seeking inspiration from abroad I had missed out on our own Arts and Crafts movement."

Although the countryside has always been part of my lifestyle. So I discovered an interest in landscape – not really knowing that it could be studied as a profession.

My time in the army (I belonged to one of the last draft intakes) was spent on the wide stretches of the Wiltshire Downs. This two-year stint gave me time to think about the future. Farming, my first choice, was out – my father wisely pointing out that we hadn't a farm, nor could we afford one – so I moved to horticulture. Commercial horticulture at the county school provided a wonderful basic grounding in plant cultivation which I have never regretted.

I went from there to a three-year apprenticeship with Nottingham Parks Department. The apprentices worked in walled vegetable gardens. We pruned peaches and vines and hoed fields of wallflowers. Later we planted traffic islands in typical Victorian mode, and lopped and pruned nineteenth-century arboretum plantings. The apprentices worked under cool glass and in steaming hothouses. We cut flowers and arranged them for civic functions and on playhouse stages. The last six months of my three-year apprenticeship were spent in the planning and design of the many aspects of, what was for the time, an advanced parks department. I began to feel my way forward, moving to London to work as a junior in the office of the garden designer Brenda Colvin. On her retirement, I went to work with Dame Sylvia Crowe and later completed my landscape training at University College, London. To broaden my design experience, I then went to work for a monthly publication – *Architectural Design*. My job at first was to redraw and simplify the architectural plans that accompanied a finished article. So I was exposed to all the best buildings – both commercial and domestic – of the 1960s and early 1970s. When it came to landscape design around the buildings, there was none. I slowly evolved a system that brought together the building with its surroundings, hence my grid system – which seemed a revelation to many. The abstract "modern" designs I was working on around the buildings were essentially to do with layout

country house tradition

TOP The style of the country house garden depended upon an informed owner, a good staff, and originally a stable providing manure to feed both the walled vegetable garden and the flower garden.

LEFT I realize in retrospect that I grew up in a world dominated by the Arts and Crafts style. The building had to have a certain mellowness, and was concealed within a lush garden, with the more roses the better! This is Jekyll's own garden at Munstead Wood.

and the basic plan – they had little to do with decorative planting, about which I was pretty ignorant. Because Britain had more or less escaped Modernism, design in any form, and particularly in the garden, was scarce. The garden was seen only as a place to show your collection of plants. It was with this background that I first started to design small town gardens in cities, including London.

From London, I moved to Oxfordshire and discovered local politics as well as village life. I have always been interested in the work of a group called Common Ground, which seeks to explore the identity of a landscape and social life within it.

There has been a romantic tradition among the British, stretching back to Wordsworth, and the eighteenth century, to do with landscape, beauty, and wildness. It is very different to the Continental tradition with regard to nature, which although superficially romantic, has more to do with mysticism. The British take a great delight in just enjoying a fine view or walking the dog in the wood or on the heath. We take this as the norm –

and have, I am quite happy to declare, a very particular regard for our countryside – and of course for the gardens within it.

Much of this concern goes hand in hand with a growing concern for the environment and its welfare, and an interest in habitat and wildlife, and with native plants and the ways in which they are distributed.

I travel a great deal and see plants that I often recognize from the garden, but growing in their own landscapes. Increasingly, I question excessive exoticism in the garden, and start to value indigenous ranges of plant material in their own particular place more highly.

New fashions in planting influence the way we use our plants. One reads now of the prairie and the steppe as models. The look created using these techniques can be spectacular, but they are for Continental-type climates, be they in North America, in Germany, or Holland. In Britain we must understand and adapt them, I believe, to make use of the huge selection of woody plants that we can grow in the United Kingdom.

natural influence

TOP An early 1970s very structured town garden that stepped up from the house to the surrounding street boundary. Intervening planting spaces are filled with grasses.

RIGHT There are few natural phenomena that can beat the breathtaking carpet of a bluebell wood in late spring. Add the sharp fragrance of their flowers, the unfurling of hazel leaves above, and the sound of the cuckoo in the distance, and this is truly paradise.

"Increasingly I question excessive exoticism in the garden, and start to value indigenous ranges of plant material in their own particular place more highly."

"Watch out, there's a new mood about...which has very little to do with plant material but everything to do with the nature of landscape."

Nowadays I sense a deeper understanding by designers of their landscapes. We are starting to see designs, large or small, that have a direct connection to their site: site-specific, a sculptor would call it. The work of the Japanese architect Tadao Ando or the Australian Glen Murcott has this feel, as does that of American garden designers and landscape architects Peter Walker, Isabelle Greene, Topher Delaney, and Kathryn Gustafson, and the late Ed Bye and Janis Hall. In Britain we have Christopher Bradley-Hole. Watch out, there's a new mood about among the new school of landscape designers, which has very little to do with plant material, at first glance, but everything to do with the nature of landscape and how the garden fits into its surroundings.

I will finish my personal journey with a quotation from a well-known American landscape architect, the late Barbara Feeley, who said that "by providing my clients with a place of beauty I am, in a spiritual sense, providing them – and myself – with the means of more closely approaching the divine". I'll buy that!

the way forward

ABOVE The work of Isabelle Greene of Santa Barbara, California, is innovative and at the same time very much of its place. This manmade swimming pool is a fine example of the sensitivity of her work.

LEFT A new mood in landscape and garden design is epitomized by Christopher Bradley-Hole's Chelsea 2000 design. It is a combination of architectural discipline, an awareness of Modernism, some essence of land art, overlaid with a natural planting style.

landscape patterns

Below the plant shapes we see around us are the underlying patterns and forms of the landscape – the rolling plains, rounded hills, or sharper mountains. In the valleys there are meandering streams and rivers, with ponds and pools to punctuate their progress. Mountain streams take a more direct route, creating a different pattern. The forces of nature mold our landscapes, shaping rounded boulders or rocky outcrops. They determine the type and look of the local soil. If the soil is waterlogged it becomes wetland. Well-drained and fertile, it may grow crops of wheat and barley, or forests of trees. These were the natural raw materials that made possible an early agricultural lifestyle.

setting

Even though a landscape may now be suburban, the ground beneath has a life of its own. It has a history, a geology, a soil. Each setting is unique.

I have outlined my own journey through garden and landscape – and will now go on to explain how those experiences and influences affect the way I create a garden. But I am conscious that there is a danger of presenting my ideas as though we all make gardens on a blank sheet of paper or isolated ground.

In theory, this is how one starts off, thinking about the facets of basic design, creating a ground pattern, spatial sequencing, making spaces, moving from space to space and so on; but the reality is that we all make gardens within a setting. It is from the feel of that setting that you evolve a pattern for your garden that is appropriate for the household that uses it. (Talking of pattern and shape, the dictionary defines pattern as a decorative design upon a surface, and shape as a total effect produced by a thing's outlines.)

The old approach to garden design was a formalized layout, which was imposed upon the site, sometimes cutting and excavating to fit the alien, often "Italianate," concept into it with a heavy hand. I think we work with our landscapes a little more sensitively now – even though the natural landscape has quite often been reduced down to much smaller scale, suburban dimensions. "But" – I hear you say – "I live in a development of similar houses, surrounded by similar fences with no outlook, how can I be sensitive to my location?" I have to agree that some developers give you little leeway. Perhaps the solution should be quite structured in this case, using the influence of the interior of the house as much as the exterior of the garden. You will be building "a room outside", perhaps repeating a wooden floor inside as decking outside, for instance. Think about using the same containers for plants inside and out, coordinating colors and fabrics. Even using mirrors to reflect an image can help. Sliding windows will facilitate the transition, as will the style of the furniture and the choice of lighting. Think "use," rather than "plant," and where you think "plant," think "specimen" rather than "flower." The sad fact is that with generations of urban living behind us we have quite often lost the ability to think organically.

the new, small garden

Lives are lived in the areas surrounding these suburban houses. Cars are parked, mail is sent, and garbage collected. Children play in the garden, and their parents mow, potter, or relax. But all these functions have to be related to the site to make them work, and it is only through the interpretation of a garden's design that they will do so. The design will be styled in a number of ways – but it is far easier to manage if it suits its setting.

city patterns

We belong to one of the first generations that are able regularly to see housing patterns from the air as we fly over them. But why do they shift in outline, color, and formation? It is all to do with the landscape in which they sit, and more interestingly the social pattern within which they are organized. Older, small-town groupings reflected social structures in the way the biggest houses had successively dwindling sizes of house around them. Newer conurbations have huge areas we call suburbs growing out in waves from the center of the city. But each of those waves of urban development has its own architectural style, and a garden style to complement it.

"...spare a moment to think what was on your land previously. Perhaps it was farmed for generations..."

It is this philosophy that allows enclosures of developers' town houses to be built surrounded by virgin countryside – only to be succeeded by other similar developments.

But spare a moment to think what was on the land previously. Perhaps it was farmed for generations – but by whom, and what did they graze or grow? What were the predators, the wildlife, and natural flora? And before cultivation, was the land natural forest or prairie land? Before agriculture, what grew there? In Europe, and indeed in most populated places around the world, old survey maps describe parcels of land, including quite often their physical characteristics and what grew there. In Britain, pub names often suggest an identity, referring to agricultural practice, "The Hop Pickers," "The Walnut Tree" and so on. These suggest the traditional agricultural identity of a location.

Then you have weather and soil to consider, both of which would have determined a possible previous building vernacular. Was rock available to build, or lumber, or only clay for making bricks or tiles for the roof? Or was it reed or rushes?

landscape patterns

TOP A foreground garden, which blends beautifully into the landscape beyond. Shrubs and perennials are arranged organically in the flower beds to enhance the smooth flow from the garden into the landscape.
LEFT Early British plowing patterns, which helped to drain the land, are revealed from the air to show a startling landscape pattern. This previous existence defines the culture of a landscape and can be used to influence a garden or landscape design.

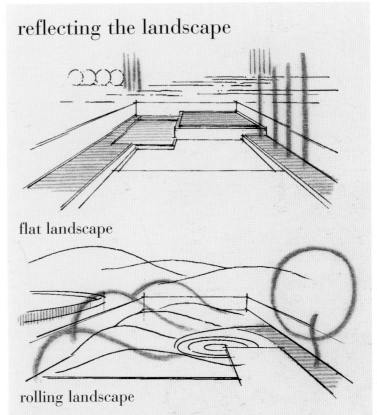

reflecting the landscape

flat landscape

rolling landscape

You would be very fortunate to have a garden in the proximity of any of the accompanying landscapes. These two sketches show how you can extract the essence of a landscape and interpret it on a smaller scale. In a flat landscape setting the checkerboard effect of agricultural pattern can be interpreted in the garden with planting used to anchor it all into the setting. In a rolling landscape, earth shaping using the excavated earth can be utilized to create rolling contours and helps to block out noise from nearby roads.

agricultural patterns

The original purpose of a garden was to grow food. Only wealthy landowners could afford to create purely decorative gardens rather than functional vegetable plots. Otherwise, garden layouts were based on the most efficient set-up for growing food. The row-by-row patterns and parterres found in early formal gardens obviously derive from the previous agricultural patterns.

Agricultural patterns overlay our landscape forms. Flatter areas were used for crop production, and forested areas covered the higher ground. The fields terraced for rice production in the Far East offer an inspiring model for sloping sites.

If your garden is in a rural setting, you should endeavor not to make it a sanctuary from the landscape, but rather a part of it. The garden design should acknowledge the neighboring agricultural practices and the planting should contain native species.

"Was rock available to build, or lumber, or only clay for making bricks?"

Again, in the U.S., areas were colonized by Swedes, by Germans, and by the Spaniards according to region. The structure of barns, and the colors in which they were painted quite often defines the origins of the people who owned them.

In both North and South America there were indigenous peoples who built in certain ways and patterned their artefacts according to the available materials.

I think that we trample over these ghosts in our landscape at our cost. We seldom pause to consider why our towns developed in a different way to another one, why they look different, and if they don't, what is the common factor? Surely some of these thoughts must define the setting not only for our gardens, but for our lifestyles as well?

I would concede that this thinking still has more to do with our artists, our conservationists, our foresters, and our landscape architects than it seems to have with our garden designers – but as I have suggested in my book *New Landscapes*, things are beginning to change (although for many people this will take a

local materials

TOP Barns were important to early settlers for storing grain and sheltering cattle. Settlers of German or Swedish extraction, often built barns using a small selection of local materials.

ABOVE Alpine structures are usually wooden because of the availability of local lumber, and they sit naturally in a wooded landscape.

RIGHT In the desert, stone and clay are available from which low-level adobe structures can be built.

> *"But even they, I think, are casting a sideways glance at the meadow and the prairie and the grassier, wilder way."*

lot of budging to change their opinion!). But even they, I think, are casting a sideways glance at the meadow and the prairie and the grassier, wilder way.

How then does one evaluate one's setting, beyond the social context I have described above? Perhaps some headings might help us define different territories: central urban, loose urban, suburban, flat rural, hilly rural, mountainous, wetland, seascape, subdesert, Mediterranean, subtropical.

Most of us are located in one of these settings, which can of course be subdivided down into moorland edge, bush, pampas, deciduous woodland, coniferous forest, and pastoral land, for example. It is the altitude and water availability that defines the soil of the area and what will grow upon it. Add to this the effect of climate, and you are describing the ecology of a landscape. These are called "unamended" landscapes. The farmed or gardened landscape has been amended, and the ground "improved" with chemicals. Increasingly, organic farming, while allowing soil amendment, allows nothing that is toxic.

natural plantings

We tend to enjoy filling our own garden landscapes with alien plants that are not native to the site. I'm not advocating that you fill it with indigenous plants – weeds we used to call them – rather that you use plant material sympathetic to the spirit of your place. Here we see wild grasses in Wales and brightly colored self-seeded meadow perennials in Turkey.

We can learn a lot about planting by looking at the surrounding landscape and the species that thrive.

It is quite often the "feeling" of a particular area that attracts us to it in the first place, and when we leave it, it is what we miss about a place. Many people are drawn to landscapes that contain water. This is not only for leisure and recreation, to swim or boat, but because water has a vernacular of its own. The watery area may be populated with sand dunes, gravel, specific plant associations, and seaside buildings. In the mountains it is the expansive views that we find exhilarating, and in the desert it is not the heat we "feel", but the beauty of this silent place.

All these differing moods are created by particular landscapes. It is often only in later life when we no longer need to be close to the city for work that we have the luxury of being able to live in the landscape. With people leaving the land to work in cities, the agricultural landscape is changing, and large tracts may revert to their natural state. As you fly over the countryside, you can see the outlines of previous civilizations. It is these "shadows" that provide the basis for research into landscape and gardens, and how previous inhabitants lived.

rural settings

TOP Forest was the natural vegetation for much of northern Europe and the east coast of North America. Little of the original forest now remains.

RIGHT Wetland areas are rich in plants and wildlife, providing important migratory rest stops during spring and fall. Much wetland has been drained for housing development and polluted by sewage.

ABOVE Village housing in a vernacular style, using reed thatch for roofs.

vernacular buildings

The natural materials available not only defined our early agricultural methods, but also the structures our ancestors built as dwellings. Was there stone available with which to build, or just clay for brick-making and for tiles? Was wood available in plenty, or did it have to be dragged for miles? In addition to these practical considerations, cultural preferences and social status defined building style, size, and position. Man's amazing inventiveness created a wealth of different vernacular idioms around the world. But regional building differences have been slowly eradicated by industrialization and improved transportation, which have made cheap materials available to all.

"The urban garden in a warm Mediterranean climate becomes an extension of the home, another room in fact."

An awareness of these factors helps to define how we use our garden space now. The urban garden in a warm Mediterranean climate becomes an extension of the home, another room in fact. Moving away from the urban center to a more relaxed setting in which it is more pleasant to bring up a family, more space is available – for a swimming pool, sauna, tennis court, and so on. For this reason, most people settle for a suburban area.

As you move into a suburban setting, environmental issues become more relevant as well – the wood, at the end of the garden and the deer living in it; the fields or open land down the road, and their rabbits.

Birds, too, enliven the space – increasingly, it is a knowledge of birds and wildlife within the suburban garden that creates this new environmental awareness of our individual settings. Each setting is unique and special – tempered only by our dogs or our cats, and what we grow. More and more we realize that native vegetation produces more food in the form of seeds and berries, and hence more wildlife that depends on it, to enliven the

the garden room

TOP For the Mediterranean gardener the arbor provides an ideal support for plant material.
LEFT Garden structures can be expressive of their location, not only in their function, but in the material of which they are built. The arbor provides an additional summer room, built of stone and wood.
RIGHT In more permanently warm climates, the loggia built into the main house becomes a fully furnished summer living room.

> *"...it is a knowledge of birds and wildlife within the suburban garden that creates this new environmental awareness of our individual settings."*

the ecology of a garden

ABOVE Where there is intensive cultivation, as in this vegetable garden, water will be necessary as well as much enrichment and improvement of the soil texture for healthy plant growth.

RIGHT Wildflowers and selected rampant climbers, along with woody plants native to the area, need little additional water and no feeding because they have adapted themselves to their location. Surely we can learn from this.

garden. Some herbs are useful – but supermarkets or farmers' markets provide vegetables without our work, and with luck they are organically grown. Of course, there are still those who want a real vegetable garden as well, though often it has to be caged in to protect it from wildlife. And you can make space for the compost bin and the bonfire – all traditional elements of the working garden.

If I live in a rural setting, be it pastoral or subdesert, do I want an emerald green lawn in summer when all the vegetation in the surrounding landscape is brown? The question of water availability in your area, and whether you need to irrigate, must temper your decisions. Vegetables need water, but there are substitutes for green lawns if you can't stand a seasonal brown one – more paving, bark mulch, gravel, or groundcover areas – or a mix. A look at your natural local groundcover will tell you a lot.

As I write this during winter 2000-2001, Britain has had one of our wettest seasons in living memory. My town of Chichester (always only a few feet above the normal water table) could

"...do I want an emerald green lawn in summer when all the vegetation in the surrounding landscape is brown?"

have been flooded if emergency piping had not been brought in to divert the flow of excessive downland water run-off. Recent agricultural techniques whereby the grass sward, which soaks up water, has been replaced by a ground tilled for winter wheat have meant that when the soil is saturated, water runs off too fast. Even my own village of Fontwell, dry for generations, has started to have springs due to land saturation, and is living up to its name again. Is this all to do with global warming? Will successive winters be as wet? Is our climate changing? We have no alternative but to adapt. We can sometimes manipulate the forces of nature, but seldom control them.

Farming and conservation techniques, which are subject to the same natural laws, also impinge upon the garden and define the setting in which we would create our gardens.

This concern for environmental issues is now becoming a strong influence on twenty-first-century garden designers. I think it is interesting to draw a parallel with the traditional Japanese garden (of which there are many sorts).

water conservation

TOP Over large outer areas of a garden in Chile, grass is still an ideal medium, which if it goes brown in drought will be in keeping with its surroundings.

LEFT The garden writer Penelope Hobhouse has eradicated much lawn. Plants self-seed in the gravel and thrive in their well-drained situation.

RIGHT A paved and graveled terrace area provides drainage close to the house. This is necessary because the house is on a lower level than the raised lawn area.

the essence of nature

LEFT A small Japanese "picture" garden, where a favorite landscape is recreated on a reduced scale. Flower color is not important, tranquility is, as you sit indoors and contemplate this quiet scene. In summer the humidity can be intense, and such a view is very cooling.

BELOW The design of larger strolling gardens is based upon landscape form and shape, though it is sometimes stylized. Trees and shrubs are encouraged by pruning and wiring to take on often exaggerated natural forms, as though blown by wind or stunted by their roots growing over rock.

Japanese influence weaves its way in and out of garden design. The 1930s not only saw many Japanese plants become commercially available, but there was a vogue for the seeming simplicity of the Japanese home, which had strong similarities to Modernism. Much of the influence came from the West Coast, because there were many Japanese living there.

Our current thoughts on creating habitat seem to mirror the Japanese idea of distilling nature down to a garden scale – they could be described as "nature-scape" rather than landscape gardens. "Macro wild" is turned into "micro garden" through the medium of rock, water, and plant life, providing on the smallest scale a tiny picture of a well-known landscape. Larger gardens encourage the Japanese viewer to explore where pond becomes metaphor for lake or even ocean.

Dry nature-scape gardens (Karescansui – the prominent style of Zen gardens) tend to be more symbolic, with an intention to

"Our current thoughts on creating habitat seem to mirror the broad Japanese idea of distilling nature down to a garden scale..."

teach through meditation. Whether the Japanese garden was intended for enjoyment alone or whether it was intended to show a deep philosophical truth through a Buddhist, Taoist, Shinto, or Confucian motif, the garden serves to open us up to taking another look at our lives in the wider perspective. This sentiment mirrors our own current position in the West where we are increasingly aware of global issues.

I think with our concerns for nature a new type of feeling for the land has begun to emerge. It is within this philosophical approach to a landscape that you start to define the shape of your garden. We will all interpret this mood our own way, and indeed we are beginning to see gardens of regional character emerging. Larger gardens used to encompass this philosophy: craftsmen could only build the local way. Nowadays, we are spoiled for choice. We can import and create instant gardens, but I think we are learning to find our own character.

natural rock formations

If you look at rock formations, you will see how climate, wind, and rain have worked to erode and sculpt the landscape, exposing different minerals and creating striking shapes. The decomposition of these minerals creates our soils and determines the soil color in our landscapes.

When working with rocks or large boulders in a garden setting, I try to reflect the natural plane and grain of the rock in the overall design. In the traditional Japanese garden, the very position of the rock within the garden setting is infused with symbolic significance.

shape

Natural influences and cultural changes affect how we look at shape in the twentieth century. Garden design now has an alternative to the classic approach.

A garden is made up of shapes – ground shape or pattern, water shape, tree shape, leaf shape, and flower shape. All these individual shapes sit within a shaped site, often rectangular, and the biggest shape – the house – sits in the middle of it. Yet the first thing many gardeners think about is flowers and how to grow them successfully. They are carried away with growing potential and a concern for plants and color. There are publications galore on the technique of cultivating plants and looking after them, but few publications on the shape of the area within which you practice the technique.

My garden design students say that once they have understood that shape comes before everything else when planning out a garden design from scratch, the scales fall from their eyes and suddenly they see shape everywhere to the exclusion of color and texture. Shape is all-important. So this is an essay on understanding shape.

The idea of a series of small shapes making up a larger pattern – the basic elements of a garden's design – rather frightens people, because it is an abstract concept when developed initially as a design drawing on paper.

shapes from flowers

It is important to learn to look. I find that sketching concentrates the mind and can be backed up by photographs. From the smallest allium flowerhead (above) to the largest umbrella or stone pine (far right), you learn to appreciate shape in nature. A garden is made up of shapes that create a tapestry.

In my own garden (right) a clipped box ball contrasts with spires of salvia and evening primrose (*Oenothera missouriensis*). This is a striking juxtaposition of shape as well as color.

plant forms as design inspiration

The beauty of plant forms is overwhelming. There is a scientific logic to their growth – a result of the plant's adaptation to its natural environment. Nothing is random in nature. Everything is honed and conditioned to optimize the plant's ability to photosynthesize and grow. We can learn lessons from this to apply to garden design. You can make many useful discoveries about shape, texture, and pattern if you take time to look carefully at plant structures and the way they grow in the garden.

*"As a formal garden style developed,
the shapes between the plots became
more important than the infill..."*

So let's get used to the idea of shapes defining a garden by looking at the development of garden layout through history. So far as we know, early cultivated plots, protected from the wild, had formal layouts for ease of cultivation. The same concept still survives today in food-providing gardens.

With the emergence of a social hierarchy, bigger garden spaces were created as symbols of affluence, and the plotted infill patterns became more elaborate. Most Italian and French Renaissance gardens are examples of this, with views controlled between the plots to form axes or avenues. As a formal garden style developed, the shapes between the plots became more important than the infill. By the time of Versailles and Vaux, it is the avenues that dominate, radiating outward from the house. Historically, these shapes then move on from being static to strongly directional.

Nineteenth-century garden shapes tend to be smaller, as history moved from gracious living toward public garden layouts and the middle-class villa garden. Although often based on formal Italianate design, the overall shape gave way to the

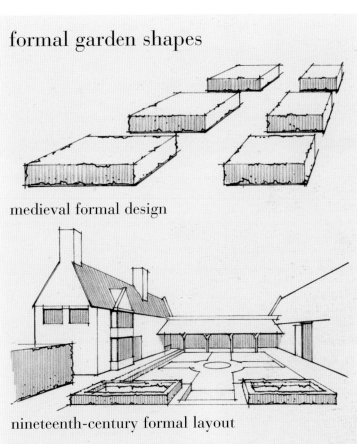

formal garden shapes

medieval formal design

nineteenth-century formal layout

The basic pattern of a small medieval plot of beds, surrounded by box hedging, was little different to the shape of a much larger classic Renaissance garden with its box-hedged parterres and avenues that form axes. Both the nineteenth-century Italianate style of garden and that of the Arts and Crafts movement reverted to the small formal layout. The Italianate style was filled with half-hardy bedding plants, and the Arts and Crafts with perennials.

grand Italianate designs

LEFT The grand seventeenth-century layout of Villa Chigi Cetinale, in Tuscany, has a broad central axis running from the house toward a steep hill and from the hill down through a massive gateway. There is a view toward the great double staircase on the western side of the house from between the avenue of cypress. On each side are grove plantings of olive trees; we see this geometry throughout the region.

> *"One of the causes of the Modernist movement was a reaction against this mish-mash which laid too much emphasis on decoration, and not enough on form or shape."*

importance of the planted infill, for we are now into the age of decorative horticulture.

Although layouts of the late nineteenth-century Arts and Crafts period in Britain were still formal, planting style became softer with the cottage garden influence. Throughout the twentieth century in Britain, plants and flowers became increasingly important to the gardener, while shape was less so.

One of the causes of the Modernist movement was a reaction against this mish-mash, which laid too much emphasis on decoration, and not enough on form or shape.

Alongside the Modernist movement in design and architecture (gardens didn't come into it much) was a whole new movement in non-representational art, culminating in Abstract Expressionism. Artists such as Mondrian, van Doesburg, and Paul Klee (and later, in Britain, Ben Nicholson) showed through their work a new world of shape and form, of color, abstraction, and dimension. The architects Le Corbusier, Rietveld, and Mendelsohn were exploring new structural shapes with new building materials so that the modern house expressed revolutionary concepts of space, organized by color and form.

This new vocabulary was as appropriate to cheaper city housing as to the gardens of the comparatively rich. However, as Jane Brown wrote in *The Modern Garden*, "To the British country house owners brought up in the faith that a great garden was a synonym for extravagance, excellence of classic design, horticultural achievement and acreage, the notion that a small garden could exhibit an equally high quality of design and planting was almost impossible to comprehend."

Of all the garden images that came from Europe between the wars, those shown at the Decorative Arts exhibition in Paris in 1925 were the most exciting. A garden designed by the architect Gabriel Guevrékian (right) attracted the most comment. The garden was a small, triangular concept of squares and zigzag shapes, a garden of water and light, with planes of colored planting constructions in colored glass. It was called a Cubist garden, Cubism being the forerunner of Abstraction.

a Cubist garden

This extraordinary Cubist garden was created by Gabriel Guevrékian in 1927 at Hyères, in the South of France. It not only heralds new design forms in the garden, but the smaller, modern garden as well. Stepped planter boxes are interspersed with paving and water to create a pattern intended to be seen from the house and terrace above. This simple design is all about shape and pattern, and has little to do with horticulture – an approach that was quite revolutionary in its time. The garden, which once belonged to the Vicomte de Noailles, was intended to be looked down upon from the house designed by Mallett-Steven. The garden has now been restored.

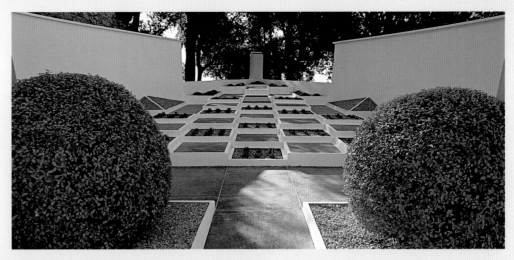

view from the house

view from terrace above

the plan

gravel borders

small pool

clipped hedges

gardens with geometry

The geometric layout does not necessarily have to be symmetrical, with the left-hand side exactly mirroring the right. Even if the underlying design has this precise balance, the planting overlay need not. Many houses and situations call for a formal approach to their design – but do not force yourself into a straitjacket.

By simply shifting one element of the formal layout when you are conceiving the design, I think you can often create a subtle juxtaposition of shapes that strengthens the appearance of the final garden layout.

The garden was reconstructed for the Vicomte de Noailles in 1927 at Hyères near Toulon and has recently been restored. The Cubist garden concept, in fact, is heavily dependent on shape, and was extraordinary for its size at the time. To us now, Guevrékian's garden is not particularly shocking, (which shows how we have moved along), but it introduced suddenly a new geometry to garden design.

My own introduction to Modernism was perhaps through the work of Ben Nicholson, to whose work I was introduced by Geoffrey Jellicoe. I think that Susan and Geoffrey Jellicoe's house in Highgate was one of the first private houses in which I saw modern art and could ask questions about it.

What appealed to me was the clarity of Nicholson's early landscape painting and a lack of what was then called "sophistication." Other British artists with a similar direction were Stanley Spencer, Henry Moore, Jacob Epstein, Frank Dobson, and Cedric Morris. Nicholson was among this new group all working together – young architects, painters, and sculptors. From early landscapes, Nicholson moved to an interest in abstraction and carved reliefs. (Geoffrey subsequently used a huge Nicholson relief in the celebrated garden he designed at Sutton Place.) These reliefs were often compared to contemporary Modernist architecture and were thought of as suitable sculptural decoration for the modern home, indicating a growing community of ideas in Britain. But the Modern Movement proper did not get to Britain until the 1930s, when the work of Le Corbusier captured the imagination of young architects. His masterpiece, the Villa Savoye at Poissy, was very influential on designers.

The flow of space from the inside to the outside of these new buildings, and the often barely perceptible change of plane, found a direct counterpart in Nicholson's reliefs, which themselves resembled walls or buildings.

It was not only Nicholson's reliefs that appealed to architects, but also his geometric color paintings of the late 1930s. His use of color had a great deal to teach architects about

concrete revolutionaries

TOP A Ben Nicholson carved relief at Sutton Place, Surrey, illustrates the clarity of his work, which was a great influence on his contemporaries. © Angela Verren-Taunt 2001. All Rights Reserved, DACS.
RIGHT Le Corbusier (1887-1965) is arguably one of the twentieth-century's greatest architects. Completed by 1931, his Villa Savoye at Poissy outside Paris was designed as a weekend house for a client. The four-square house is raised above its site on columns. The architect described the house as "a machine for living in." © FLC/ADAGP, Paris and DACS, London 2001.

"The flow of space from the inside to the outside of these new buildings, and the often barely perceptible change of plane, found a direct counterpart in Nicholson's reliefs, which themselves resemble walls or buildings."

design dictated by site

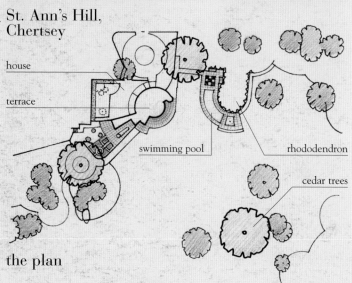

St. Ann's Hill, Chertsey

house

terrace

swimming pool

rhododendron

cedar trees

the plan

Described as "the most complete ensemble of modern house and garden in Britain" (Jane Brown in *The Modern Garden*), St. Ann's Hill, Chertsey, was built between 1936-38 by the architect Raymond McGrath and the landscape architect Christopher Tunnard. The basic design motif was a circle, inspired by the shapes of the cedar trees in the grounds as seen by the client from his airplane. In the design, a sheltered courtyard radiates out from the house. A second semicircle faces the house, encircling a swimming pool that encloses a magnificent rhododendron. Viewed at roof level, the house becomes a sculpture of shapes in the landscape. This 1930s project encapsulates much of what postWar garden and landscape design was all about – design dictated by site.

space. And space as opposed to classic decoration was what much of Modernism was all about.

Many of the influences of modern design in architecture, in painting, and in sculpture, were brought together in a book by Christopher Tunnard in 1938 entitled *Gardens in the Modern Landscape*, in which he sought to give the garden architect a way forward through the use of order and shape.

To give examples for his theory, he illustrated his collaboration with the architect Raymond McGrath. The design and landscape of a new house at St. Ann's Hill, Chertsey, in Surrey was realized between 1936-1938. The plans of house and garden were developed together on an eighteenth-century site. The house occupied more than half of the circular plan, and the south front was completed with a curving paved terrace. The flowing geometry of the garden is genuinely new. It even had a swimming pool, curving around a huge rhododendron bush. This concept of a sculpture of shapes within the natural landscape was electrifying at the time.

overlapping surfaces

RIGHT In looking at some of the work of the contemporary American landscape architect Martha Schwartz (in this case an office-complex roof garden), I am reminded of the shapes of a Nicholson relief and his geometric paintings (top). There is a harmony in this sculptural composition; the stone, marble, and gravel are successfully combined with young tree planting. The scale fits the building superbly – demonstrating unity of buildings and site.

a Modernist solution

The architectural partnership of Mendelsohn and Chermayeff began in 1933. When Mendelsohn was working abroad, his partner decided to build a house at Halland in Sussex between 1934-1958, called Bentley Wood. This house became an icon of preWar Modernism. The concept of house and garden – which were inseparable – sat within a light planting of birch trees. Christopher Tunnard, Chermayeff's landscape architect, used a precise cast-concrete paving to give a grid perspective echoed in the screen behind. The detail of steps and sculpture plinth was exciting, too, offering a pared-down Modernism. Henry Moore thought his figure "to be a kind of focal point for all the horizontals." He later recalled: "The sculpture had its own identity and did not need to be on Chermayeff's terrace, but so to speak enjoyed being there…a mediator between a modern house and ageless land."

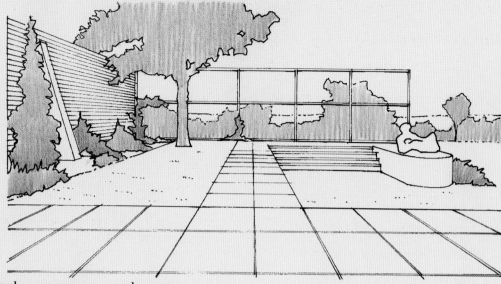

the concrete paved terrace

view from the house toward the open screen

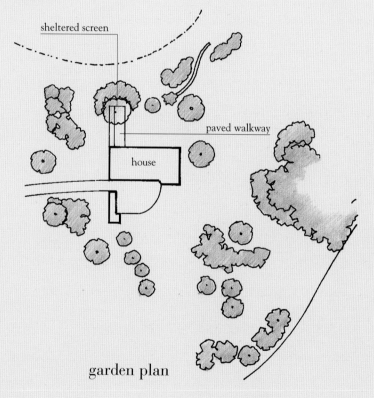

garden plan

recumbent figure 55

The organic form of a Henry Moore reclining figure provides the ideal punctuation mark when it is seen against a natural backdrop of rolling countryside. Indeed, Moore was inspired by the shapes of flint stones he found in the surrounding chalk downland.

> *"Eckbo's appreciation of space, the three-dimensional experience – he draws a garden as a roofless box – allied him to artists and sculptors..."*

A year or two before St. Ann's Hill, Chertsey (1936-1938), the architect Erich Mendelsohn had built himself a new house near Halland in East Sussex, using the young Christopher Tunnard as his landscape architect. The house was flat-roofed, with fully glazed and sliding windows that faced the garden. It looked south, with a view to the downs across a level, paved terrace. One arm of this terrace pushed out into the landscape, terminating in an open screen. Against this, and balanced by an existing oak tree, Tunnard sited a Henry Moore sculpture, entitled "Recumbent Figure." This pre-World War II simple set piece was a classic of Modernist integrated design for my generation of postWar students, and was illustrated in Tunnard's book.

When Tunnard moved to teach at Harvard in 1938, his reputation, based on the book, preceded him.

What Tunnard taught and wrote about was the concept of working with nature. Nothing new in that; Jekyll and Robinson were very nearly contemporary and had lived within fifty miles or so of Halland. But Tunnard, with the advent of plate glass,

brought the garden into the house and vice versa, as he had demonstrated at Halland. The concept became as one with the volume of a room and the volume of a garden appearing as a unified sequence of three-dimensional spaces.

Two American designers took forward Tunnard's influence in their work – Thomas Church (1902-1978), my guru, and Garret Eckbo (1910-1999).

Michael Laurie, who was knowledgeable about the Cubist and Bauhaus design movement of Europe, and edited the 1948 edition of Thomas Church's book *Gardens are for People*, said of Church's work: "He goes beyond the mere satisfaction of requirements, and into the realms of fine art."

Garret Eckbo's appreciation of space, the three-dimensional experience (he conceived a garden as a roofless box), allied him to artists and sculptors as well. He extended this theory into the "ultimate aesthetic possibilities" of materials. For the garden he named the four fundamentals of earth, plant, rocks, and water – "the technique of earthwork is engineering, but its concept of

a box without a roof

TOP A Garret Eckbo garden which embodies much of the sculptural philosophy of his period. He felt that a garden was a box without a roof, and the elements of his layout he saw as individual units that allowed him to organize the space three-dimensionally, very much as we would furnish a room. Eckbo moved from early garden design through to housing pattern and subsequently became a town planner.

"A garden, if you think about its plan from above, is a series of shapes – of grass, of water, and of planting"

form should be completely sculptural, a three-dimensional modeling, to produce the more expressive form…"

Eckbo put his theory into practice. He saw rocks as three-dimensional forms, the fundamental objects, and water as their complimentary plastic and expressive element. Planting he saw as an arrangement of individual units of infinite variety and form, color, and texture. Plant groupings organized space and made three-dimensional compositions akin to those produced by painters and sculptors. All other materials had to be subordinated to these four primary materials, or the organic integration of man with nature was lost. Garret Eckbo used his early theories when developing housing plans and then took these ideas further in his largescale landscape architecture projects.

Above all, the garden was the connecting point between man and nature.

Garden and landscape design influences came thick and fast during the early and middle parts of the twentieth century for those designers who chose to acknowledge them and experiment with these new ideas in their work. It was to these influences that I and my generation of landscape designers were heir.

Much of this early modern landscape design theory passed into landscape architecture before the growing interest in environmental issues. Garden design as a profession started to emerge in its own right in the 1960s, and the increasing awareness of the possibilities of garden design as a profession throughout the latter part of the twentieth century created a need for training in the subject.

A garden, if you think about its plan from above, is a series of shapes – of grass, of water, and of planting, all relating both to the boundary and to the house in the midst of it all. Even on a small scale, the shapes can be formalized, as in the French garden, for instance, or they can be fluid, as in those of Burle Marx (top) or Thomas Church (see page 18). The great thing is that we have the choice.

Increasingly, I feel that garden shapes should have a relationship to the pattern of their surroundings – and the larger

shapes from above

TOP The fluid organic shapes of a garden by Roberto Burle Marx in Brazil. Homogeneity was accentuated by the use of indigenous plants which the designer collected himself and propagated.

LEFT The shape of a landscape as seen from the air can give a clue to its contours, and this can be further enhanced by an agricultural pattern over it. Can this be a clue also to the sort of curving shapes we might use in the new more fluid organic-shaped garden?

shapes in a small garden

These overlapping shapes might be a basic plan of the same garden layout, with the house at the bottom, a shed or storehouse to the left behind it, with a path leading up the garden, perhaps to a small greenhouse or vegetable patch, and a further shed. It might be an early exercise in garden design and help you to start thinking about space and the relationship of areas to one another.

PLAN 1 Has a more or less traditional layout with the pattern defining what might be areas of terrace, of gravel, and of lawn, with some vegetables at the top, and then surrounded by planting against a fence – but they are all just "shapes" at this stage.

PLAN 2 Moving the shapes around, removing a constricting path, and simplifying the overall composition.

PLAN 3 Abstracting the pattern perhaps to create a more private central lawn shape surrounded with plants. The circular shape could be a pond.

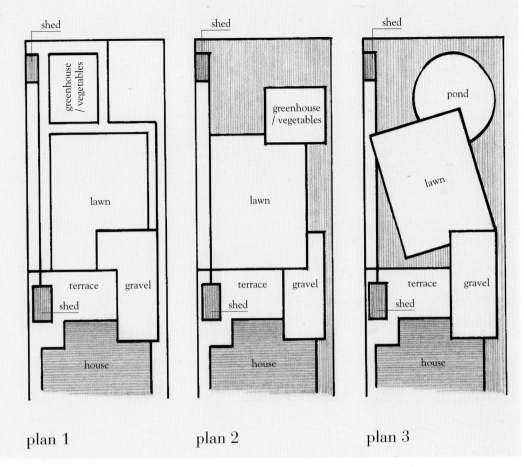

plan 1

plan 2

plan 3

they are, the more this is so. I am made aware of this when flying over landscapes – we are one of the first generations to be able to do this. Different agricultural patterns, field patterns, and housing patterns define the aerial look of different areas. Surely the gardens should follow suit? Particularly distinctive from above are golf course shapes (especially sandtraps and irrigated greens) and swimming pools – the color of the latter more than anything else. Gardens could have a similar impact and have a more beneficial effect on the environment.

Selecting the type of shape for a particular location is hugely important. If the topography isn't flat, for instance, it's possible to let the change in levels and the shape of contours inspire you. A two-dimensional design exercise therefore starts with just moving shapes about within a perimeter. Ultimately the plan for a garden will become three-dimensional as the shapes take on a form or bulk, and as you define what they are. Eventually, a garden design becomes an exercise in mass and void, built up from the interrelationship of elements of a scaled ground pattern.

gardens with organic shapes

The pattern of gardens that use organic shapes is often dictated either by pre-existing contours or features. The organic shape follows a rolling ground form or works through and around what is there already. It may also simulate landscape patterns – the flow of a meandering stream, a wildlife path, or coastline – or the growth pattern of natural vegetation. Organic shapes offer a relaxed style of garden design, but the designer needs to bear in mind that an element of asymmetrical balance may be needed, to create a sense of unity.

The organic or kidney shape of a swimming pool within a more formal layout can be uncomfortable – organic shapes need to work together. This is why a garden with curves suits a hilly landscape.

Make your curves strong. A thin wiggle looks simply like a crooked straight line. Look at natural plant forms – you will see that they are generally strong and bold.

evolving a module from the proportions of the house

I have taken three house facades as my example – you can measure your own by running a tape measure along the wall and reading off the running measurements of wall, window, wall, door, wall, and so on. I have shown the grid I evolved in perspective to clarify my point – you can plot your grid straight on plan (see page 83) with no perspective. This way you make a workable graph on which to begin designing your garden. Remember that grids are always square.

plan 1

Just looking at this simple elevation, you can see a visual rhythm between window and wall. With your tape measure on site and your scale on paper, note down the equal distances between the house features to create your grid or module on plan.

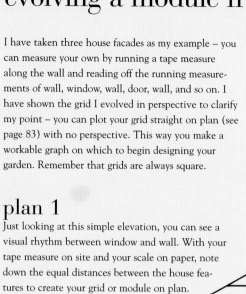

plan 2

The grid starts from the studio extension with a grid line on each side of the building and another line down the middle. I would use the same grid proportion on the left-hand side of the building as well.

plan 3

Again looking at the elevation of the glass extension, I can see that the rhythm of glass to wood areas isn't quite regular. But with a bit of adjustment on plan, I can evolve a visually satisfactory grid that will act as a guide for the ultimate design.

"The average house sits squarely upon its often rectangular plot. My basic grid exercise works off the house to mirror its proportions..."

There has to be a framework when you are evolving a design. I take it from the proportions of the house which the garden surrounds. If you don't, the scale of elements in the garden may look at odds to the scale of the house, or bits of it. If you look at the plan of the ground floor of a house, you will see that there is a relationship between the proportions of the main rooms. Look closer and you will discover the module (the basic unit of measurement) on which the architect has evolved the building.

The module is not necessarily standard. If you use this module as the basis for your garden design, it must have a proportional relationship to the house as you progress out into the garden. If you double and treble that basic grid proportion, it will allow the garden pattern you evolve within it to expand while staying in proportion to your view – or even to the height of a dominating tree.

Once you have the hang of moving shapes into a satisfactory design, you need to take the design to the next practical stage, making the geometry of your design work.

Garden and landscape patterns need to be simple and open, for practicality's sake. Think about moving around the finished garden concept on a mower, for instance. Plants tend to be circular in outline and do not fit into tight triangular areas unless they are clipped. Cutting regular squares of, say, stone or precast concrete slabs, into odd angles costs extra money. And of course, water shapes are generally broad and open.

To achieve this practical openness, start with high-school geometry and learn to use a scale. The process can be transferred to your computer if you prefer – but you have to know the rules first.

The average house sits squarely upon its often-rectangular plot. My basic grid exercise works off the house to mirror its proportions – so the garden shapes you explore should start using a right angle, working off the house at 90°.

Working on tracing paper and to scale (not too large at first), make a site plan, defining the areas by function. So, for example, decide where you want the terrace – in sun or shade –

> *"This grid concept of evolving a garden pattern is a guide to get the designer thinking about the proportional relationship between the elements of his basic shapes."*

and where you want to grow herbs (usually near the kitchen). Draw lines for paths from the house to the garage, to the rear entrance, to the trash cans, and so on. Write a brief to yourself of the functional elements you need. Every site will be different.

Over this "what-element-goes-where" sheet, start defining squared shapes, working a pattern out from the house using the proportions of the grid, though not necessarily sticking rigidly to it. As you move away from the house, let your shapes become larger – building up the size of your pattern while keeping it as multiples of the basic grid size (right).

What you will define are areas of paving, of grass, or of water – what is left over will probably be the planting, which will frame and surround your concept.

Your patterns can overlap as well – a technique I use to make a small level change, for instance. You will end up with a fairly rigid concept, which in a tight urban area might be totally appropriate. Let your paths overlay and work with your pattern. If you let paths define your pattern from the outset, you will find that you have a garden in the left-over spaces between the paths.

Using the same technique, working out from the house using right angles, introduce the circle – perhaps as a lawn or a pond. By all means add more circular areas if you have the space. This technique uses the circle in the same geometry as the square – the circle will fit within one square of the grid – or multiples of it.

Remember, areas outside your pattern are for plants. If you work from the outside in, you will get the feel of your design. If these techniques are too precise for you, start working with an octagonal shape, still working within the grid. This can create a striking honeycomb sort of effect (see pages 86-87). If the layout becomes too full of sharp angles, eradicate the awkward corners (which in reality might be impractical in a garden anyway).

While circular patterns do not generally relate to building structures, the octagon will, having some flat sides that have more in common with the walls of a building than with the contours of a landscape.

designs based on a grid

I have taken a grid or module from the garden-side elevation of a house. I have used the basic plan of the house to determine the proportions for the grid. The grid can continue around the house. I am beginning to evolve a formal pattern with a small avenue of fruit trees (right). If the client preferred something soft and curvaceous then the design (below left) would be better. Note that circles and segments of circles will all fit into the grid. The design (below right) is slightly abstracted, with a large terrace area, which might include a pool and a neighboring lawn area.

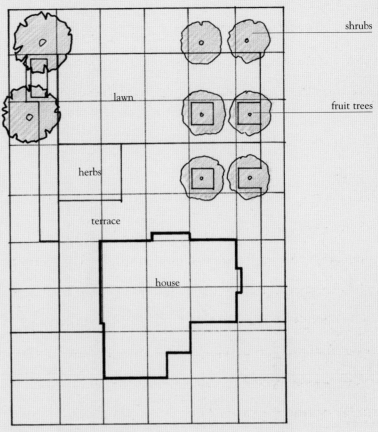

shrubs

fruit trees

lawn

herbs

terrace

house

formal design

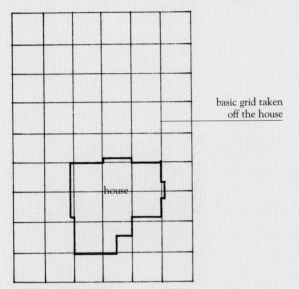

basic grid taken off the house

house

initial grid

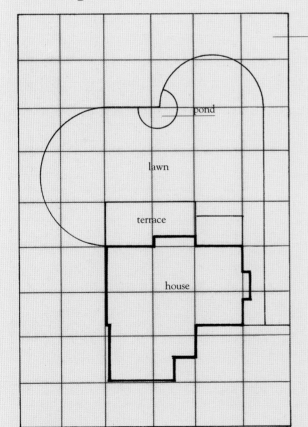

planted area

pond

lawn

terrace

house

a flowing design

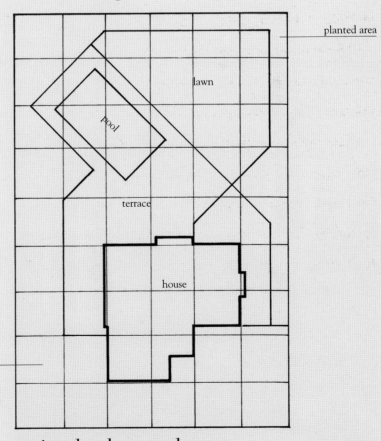

planted area

lawn

pool

terrace

house

planted area

a simple abstract layout

formal town garden

This townhouse in South London had, at some stage, a new dining-room extension (with garden doors) added at a lower level to the main house. A small retained terrace onto which the living room opens divides the extension from the conservatory. The tall and imposing rear elevation of the house needed a strong horizontal line to anchor the house to its site. The clients wanted another paved terrace and eating-out area close to the dining-room doors to the garden. This quieter space needed to be separated from the rest of the lawned garden in which their children might play.

planning the grid

As the basic grid measurement I have taken the width of the dining-room extension (the most obvious architectural feature), which is also the same dimension as that from the edge of the dining room to the center of the living-room doors. You can halve or quarter this basic measurement – it doesn't matter, but the bigger your basic module, the simpler the scale of your plan.

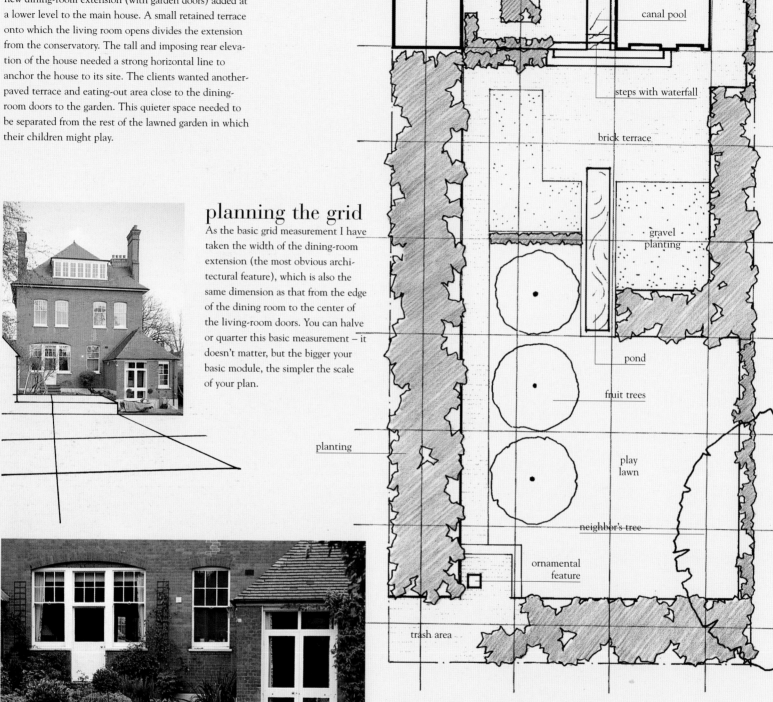

conservatory · *living room* · *kitchen window* · *dining room* · *canal pool* · *steps with waterfall* · *brick terrace* · *gravel planting* · *pond* · *fruit trees* · *play lawn* · *neighbor's tree* · *ornamental feature* · *planting* · *trash area*

the finished result

LEFT Crossing the horizontal line of steps (linking the dining room to the upper terrace) is a canal-shaped pool. The water falls over the steps and then appears again as a feature of the private terrace area. The pattern of shapes is very linear and is reinforced by a brick path running down the garden, punctuated with fruit trees.

plan on the grid

ABOVE The continuous horizontal line created by the steps and the waterfall running from the house along the dining-room wall extension creates a visual link between house and garden. In the foreground is a brick terrace with a gravel area for planting. The canallike pond is edged with brick, making a clean mowing edge for ease of maintenance.

Once you have grasped this technique, start to look at other landscape drawings, particularly those of the people about whom I have written – and then have another look at mid-twentieth century non-representational art and see how they use pattern. Bridget Riley plays optical games, Mondrian is geometricity, Rothko uses broad plains of color, and so on. It's the technique you are looking at – never mind the merit or idea! Think, too, about industrial pattern, and look for the repetition of the same manufactured forms (see Direction pages 92-111).

You can start to abstract a pattern as long as you stick to the above rules, and even mix the types of pattern.

When you are working on a larger scale – with a rural or wilder backdrop – look closely at natural pattern. I have already mentioned agricultural patterns, but now look at river patterns, meandering when sluggish and straighter when fast. Look at curves in the landscape and the river pattern – you will realize that here is a natural geometry as well. The forces of nature that mold a landscape create not only smooth land patterns but

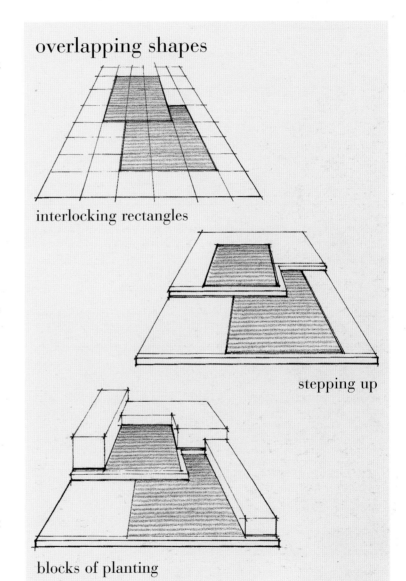

overlapping shapes

interlocking rectangles

stepping up

blocks of planting

As soon as you start to think beyond the basic plan to considering level change and block plantings, you are starting to think three-dimensionally, and this is a great step forward. I have illustrated this in the three diagrams above. The top is the two-dimensional plan of interlocking rectangles. (I have shown this in perspective – you would draw it flat, on a grid (see page 84). The center diagram shows how these could in reality be two areas of water or of grass – it depends upon the scale on which you are working. In the bottom plan I have added masses of plant material in block form to build up the design and to give the site shelter and to enclose the site visually.

using octagonal shapes

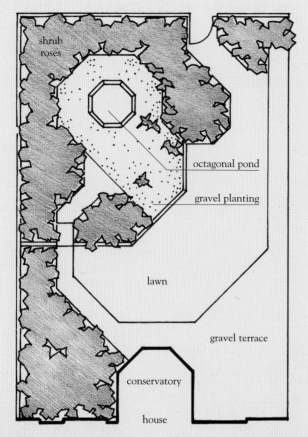

shrub roses

octagonal pond

gravel planting

lawn

gravel terrace

conservatory

house

the plan

using the conservatory shape

TOP The idea for this octagonal garden was inspired by the shape of a conservatory that was built onto the back of the house. A gravel path and terrace surround the end of the garden and the conservatory, and lead up two steps to a pond garden surrounded by shrub roses. It is a sort of oyster with the pond as the pearl.

ABOVE Not as ambitious or exotic as the garden plan (top), a hexagon design was used as the geometric shape to create a gravel path across the lawn area. This garden design idea was probably inspired by the hexagonal shape of the conservatory adjoining the house. The garden path creates a visual link between house and garden.

"While circular patterns do not generally relate to building structures, the octagon will."

different mountain and hill profiles also, some quite exaggerated, others of rounded swelling forms.

When I reach this stage, if I have a garden to design that has a landscape backdrop, I find it very difficult to create shapes that have a large enough scale to reflect the landscape without blocking the view. Obviously plant material is a great connector of gardens to landscape, but it is shape that really does it.

I found that I could create Thomas Church-type curves – although he was a great one for just simple geometry – or Roberto Burle Marx-type patterns, by doubling and trebling the size of my grid as I got to a site boundary, making me use bigger patterning in scale as I moved away from the house.

Use as many right angles (90° angles) as possible. Certainly allow lines running into a boundary or a structure to come in at that angle. Less of an angle creates a stingy shape – an ungenerous proportion. When combining a circular shape and a rectangular one, use the radii from the center of the circle as the

octagonal details

Again, it was a new conservatory that inspired this stepped terrace concept leading up to a summerhouse. The conservatory doors extend beyond this photograph and the plan shown below, so from inside the structure you get an almost ground-level view of a terrace with pots upon it, stepping up to a higher brick terrace. The hexagonal paved areas are laid in the same brickwork as the top and bottom terraces, but then in-filled with paved concrete, brushed to expose the aggregate, so the surface looks more like gravel.

Near the conservatory you will notice that the strict hexagonal shapes get elongated to fit in with other architectural features. These hexagonal shapes still have a flow to them, but their straight sides also acknowledge the surrounding flat-faced walls of the house. Walls do, of course, become softened by plant material in time, as do steps with pots of annuals, but it is the underlying design that holds the layout together, and the selection of paving materials that creates a unified design.

octagonal-shaped levels

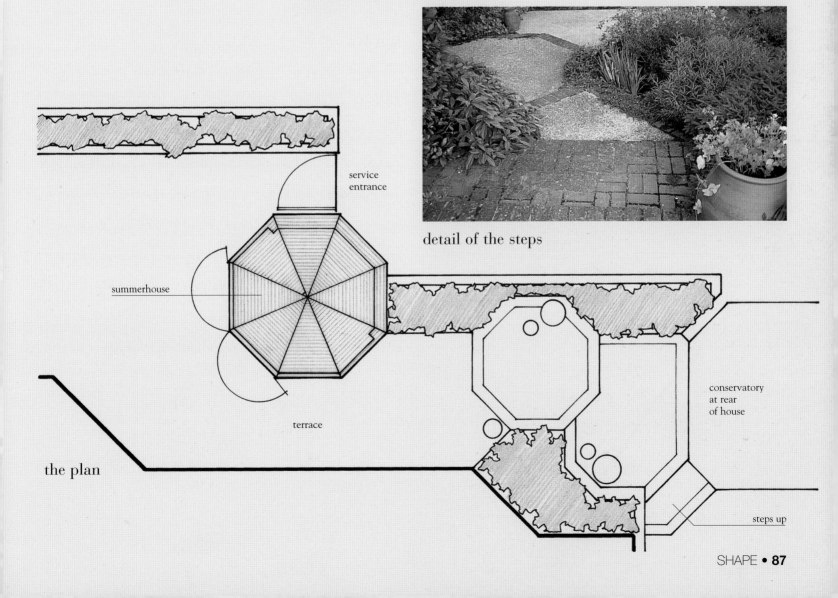

detail of the steps

service entrance

summerhouse

terrace

conservatory at rear of house

the plan

steps up

"When you are working on a larger scale – with a rural or wilder backdrop – look closely at natural pattern."

working on a larger scale

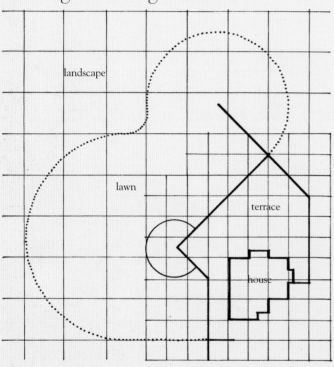

To achieve bigger, bolder curves double or even treble the grid proportions. Begin from the house and work out into your landscape. Use the geometry of the circle – its radii, for instance – to bind the curve back into the more right-angled geometry of the terrace outline and house. This technique produces, I believe, great sweeping curves that have a strong affinity with the shapes of the natural landscape (see pages 28-29). Gardens of this scale with this simple treatment are also easy to maintain with ride-on machinery, since there are no tight corners to be negotiated.

defining line. At other times, use the circumference of your circle and continue in a straight line from there.

As you construct your shapes (using the grid as a guide), give each line a logic. Do not break the logic of the concept by introducing a random free shape – give the free shape a logic. By following these broad outlines, your shapes start having a structural and proportional logic to match that of the house they surround. Wiggly hose shapes lack this logic (though admittedly they are easier to create) but it's the lazy man's way of doing it, and the result is usually all too obvious.

You will be amazed at how your design shape looks in reality on site. Walk through your embryo garden, making sure you have enough room for a terrace. Will it catch the sun where you have placed it? Is the path wide enough? Is the bed thick enough where needed to block a view? And so on.

It is probably only when you have set out your shapes on the site that you will realize there are level changes and that you may have to introduce retaining walls and/or steps.

curving landscape shapes

TOP Working in the endlessly flat pampas regions of Argentina, I could put into practice design exercises evolved on paper with no particular worries about changes in level. This curving design evolved from the technique shown in the diagram (above). It curves out into its landscape and is defined by mown and natural areas of grass.

a rolling, urban garden

This house in upstate New York, was originally the stable of a turn-of-the-century mansion that was later demolished. The house had looked into the rolling greenery of an Olmstead Park. So rather than having the garden design roll up to the park, the park had to roll down to the house, with a contoured extension to screen a boundary wall on the right-hand side of a newly-aligned driveway and forecourt. Bold, curving masses of plant material are in scale with the grassy sward and trees beyond. Simplicity was important, as was an uninterrupted view into the park beyond. The ability to clear winter snow from the drive was essential.

When working with contoured shapes, it is important to remember the practicality of good drainage, particularly in regions where there is heavy snowfall and subsequent melt. The simple shapes of the design will make the clearance of snow by machine more straightforward.

The line of the curved retaining wall at one end of the forecourt echoes the line of the bay window, which looks out onto it from the house.

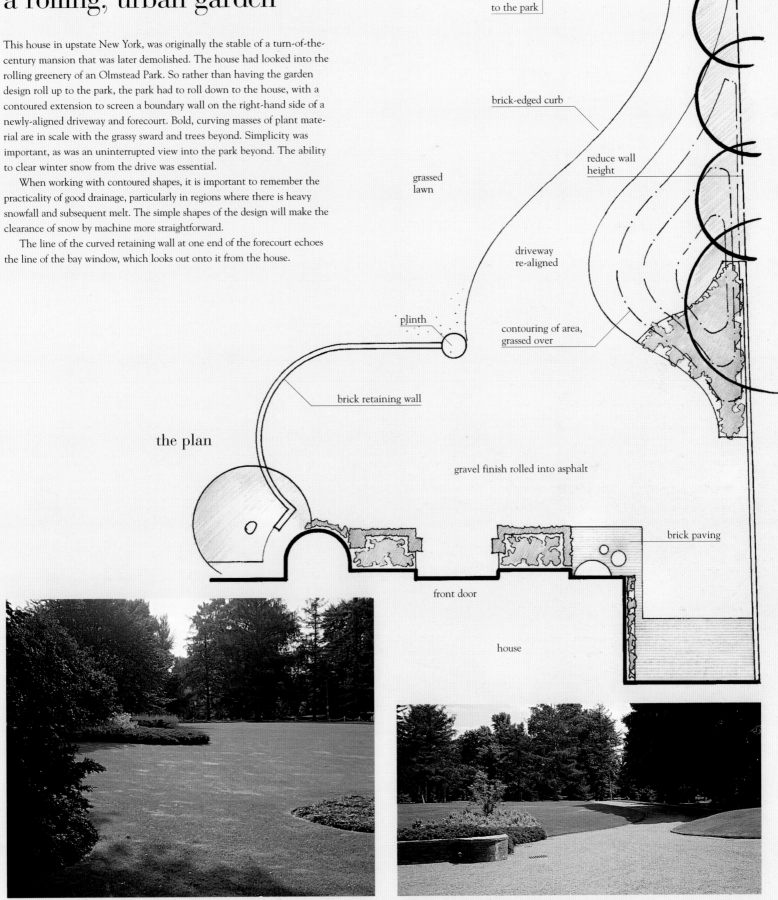

to the park

brick-edged curb

reduce wall height

grassed lawn

driveway re-aligned

plinth

contouring of area, grassed over

the plan

brick retaining wall

gravel finish rolled into asphalt

brick paving

front door

house

curving beds of plant material

sweeping gravel driveway

3

direction

A strong directional design in the classic manner is balanced, and focuses the eye; but formality can be asymmetric as well – it is another sort of balance.

For many of us, the term direction when applied to the garden probably means the line of a path to the front door or the sweep of a drive, if you have a garden large enough.

But that is thinking purely in terms of hard materials and physical movement. What about grassy lawns planted on either side with trees – the avenue – which creates a strongly three-dimensional directional route? And what about sequence – the repeat of features on a plan to create a visual rhythm that leads the eye along a line, whether straight, curved, or diagonal? On a large or small scale, direction is a key consideration for garden designers, both from the practical point of view of getting from point A to point B, but also to give a feeling of movement on the ground and in three dimensions.

But if your spade is poised to break ground, just hang on. Let's go back to the avenue, a garden feature that dates as far back as classical antiquity. The positioning of columns or trees to direct your approach to the site (or, in reverse, from within the site to out) is always a sign of authority, for the result is manmade, an unnatural plant arrangement that stamps human will upon surrounding nature. The same can be said, of course, of any formal garden layout.

The avenue of trees will inevitably focus on or frame a view. In seventeenth-century England it became known as the vista, which could equally be a sequence of openings. This is the point in the history of landscape design when the enclosed medieval plot opened out and the spaces between the cultivated areas became more important than the plots themselves (see page 65). Add more than one enclosure to another, like a string of beads, and you create direction. The enclosures may get bigger toward the horizon and so open out to it, or they may get smaller to create a more intimate, confined impression.

This interrelationship of spaces formed the basis of the Renaissance garden, often across an incline in Italy, normally more or less flat in France. In Britain, many of the formal gardens created from this post-medieval directional principle were swept away in the eighteenth century by the landscape

the avenue approach

The classic formal avenue of trees can be very beautiful, casting cool shade as you walk beneath it. Such a strong directional pull needs either a view at the far end or a sculptural feature as a full stop. This scale is too large for the smaller garden, but it can be reinterpreted using smaller trees, shrubs, or even clipped forms of box or yew. Indeed, a bed on either side of a path planted with lavender or catnip creates exactly the same effect on a reduced scale.

"We passed lines of clipped horse chestnuts along tracks and avenues, bristling double and triple rows of Lombardy poplars used as windbreaks, endlessly expanding webs of orchards and vineyards thrown over undulating contours..."

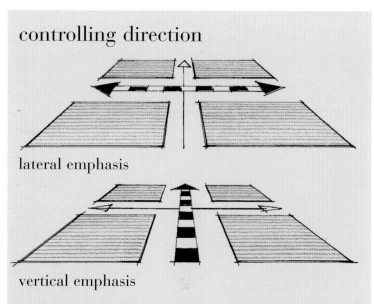

controlling direction

lateral emphasis

vertical emphasis

By widening or narrowing an existing axial direction, the garden designer can control the space and how it is used by the visitor. In the illustrated diagram (top), the dominant axis runs left and right. Somehow we expect the axis to run from the bottom of the garden to the top: we are more comfortable with this. Here, the wider path could signify a main thoroughfare in the garden, the narrower path one of less significance to the garden visitor.

Introduce perspective and the directional intention is strengthened, but the garden designer can play with this, too. Make the path wider at the far end and you visually shorten the view from one end of the path to the other. In reverse, make your actual path dimensions diverge, and you will make the space from one end of the path to the other appear deceptively longer, which is particularly useful in a smaller-scale garden where space is limited. Placing a piece of modern or traditional sculpture, or even an item of garden furniture, such as a bench, at the end of a directional path will also help to emphasize the effect of perspective, leading the eye in that direction.

style of Lancelot "Capability" Brown (1716-83). Humphrey Repton, who succeeded him, was not quite so ruthless, and slowly the formal garden was reintroduced as a series of planted areas.

It was the restrictions of this strongly directional approach to garden planning that the newer designers of the modern movement objected to. They urged a need to reinterpret: "...the rule of stiff symmetries and an insistence on design rules of a Beaux Arts faculty set forth in collections of dusty lantern slides," wrote the mid-twentieth-century designer Dan Kiley in his book *In His Own Words*.

Garret Eckbo and James Rose of the California school were the first garden designers to shuffle the forms of the formal garden, abstracting their layouts and breaking the formal tradition that had gone back as far as ancient Egyptian avenues of sphinxes.

But this geometric order of space was too tried-and-tested to be rejected entirely, as Dan Kiley – of the same school as Garret Eckbo, James Rose, and Thomas Church – discovered in his European travels of the late 1940s.

linear planting

The evolution of the formal layout probably started
with Middle Eastern irrigational channels and linear
plantings that were fed by the channels. In Europe,
irrigation was not necessary, though the directional
planting of orchards and vineyards continued for ease
of maintenance and harvesting. Formal decorative
planting, whether in city or garden, was the
next logical step.

avenues

An avenue or allée – they are the same thing – is simply a formal walk bordered by trees. The idea of the avenue is as old as garden-making, and it was the most common early sign that man was imposing order upon a natural landscape. From Persian and Roman gardens to Renaissance Italy, the seventeenth-century French gardens of Le Nôtre and on to town planning, the avenue has always had a place in formal design. The renewed interest in formality in the garden has encouraged people to plant avenues again, often with smaller trees than previously – the cypress in Italy, the hornbeam in France, the elm or linden tree in Britain.

"...sequence slows down direction, but by repetition it carries the eye forward. It is no longer classical – the rigid plan has been shattered, or rather an alternative has been evolved".

forms of sequence

avenue or allée

The avenue or allée of trees planted in two parallel rows was originally grown this way for maintenance. It was later reinterpreted as a ceremonial way.

arbor

The arbor (or garden version of the above) provides a support for climbers and shade for people walking beneath. It has been used since the earliest times in garden design.

sequential rooms

This idea of creating sequential rooms made of clipped hedges was probably borrowed from the progress through state rooms in a palace.

formal meander

The "formal meander" is a garden concept that aims to break up the length of the perimeter hedge, creating a rhythm that can be plain or infill planted.

In Dan Kiley's book *In His Own Words*, he wrote, "What I saw in the fields and forests, town plazas and streets was a language of form used to conduct the movement of daily life. We passed lines of clipped horse chestnuts along tracks and avenues, bristling double and triple rows of Lombardy poplars used as wind breaks, endlessly expanding webs of orchards and vineyards thrown over miles of undulating contours, miles of irrigational channels. In these orders and organizations of pastoral Europe…were landscapes of sustenance and ego. What opened my eyes…to the act of designers was the spatial and compositional power of these simplest of elements – this was no less than living architecture. By means of strong directional responses to existing conditions the built landscape of forms, cities and industries I saw immediately and forever displaced arbitrary formulas from my mind."

This shows an interesting development from a rejection of the formal Beaux Arts approach to landscape, through observation of agricultural and urban patterning in Europe into contemporary landscape and garden design in the United States.

using repetition

In the Miller garden in Columbus, Ohio, Dan Kiley combines the traditional European avenue, planted with honey locust, with a grid taken from the proportions of the house. The avenue culminates in Henry Moore's seated woman. The clarity and simplicity of this composition is Kiley's most powerful statement of how to design with ground cover, trees and shrubs, space and light. Repetition is not boring here – it is soothing beyond measure.

direct paths

There is more to designing a path than just creating a hard surface on which to walk, as this selection of photographs shows. A boundary of plant material, an avenue of trees, some clipped box hedging, or an architectural structure on either side (or extending over the top) create strong direction in a garden design. You can use a feature at the end of the path, like a plant in a container, to create a visual full stop. But if the path turns a corner or disappears into shadow, the full stop is not necessary. Try to avoid paving patterns that are too strong. They can interrupt the visual journey – and it is this journey along the path that really matters.

"Some of the most interesting small formal garden layouts from the middle part of the twentieth century have been constructed in Holland: formal, perhaps, though not necessarily traditional."

Dan Kiley introduces us not only to modern directional design again, but to the importance of sequence as well. It could be said that sequence slows down direction, but by repetition it carries the eye forward. It is no longer classical – the rigid plan has been shattered, or rather an alternative has evolved. Dan Kiley takes us full circle, though he achieves a very different look in the geometry of his layouts. But the scale on which Dan Kiley works is far larger than the average domestic garden – though from it you see the value of repetition more generally.

There has been a revival of interest in the directional garden of formal shapes (if indeed traditional gardeners ever abandoned it), but in Britain it has taken on some of the characteristics of the French provincial garden, albeit on a smaller scale, with box borders sometimes replaced by lavender, and the pattern infilled with roses, white preferably. Add anything clipped, set in pots, and you have the look of the fashionable urban garden in Britain.

European influence

In this part of Mien Ruys' demonstration garden at Dedemsvaart in Holland, she has abstracted box masses, allowing the feel of a formal small garden, but softened by lush accompanying planting. Born in 1904, Mien Ruys had met the aged Gertrude Jekyll at Munstead Wood, her own garden in Britain, and knew of Christopher Tunnard's work as well. Mien Ruys was an enormous influence on the development of modern garden design in northern Europe.

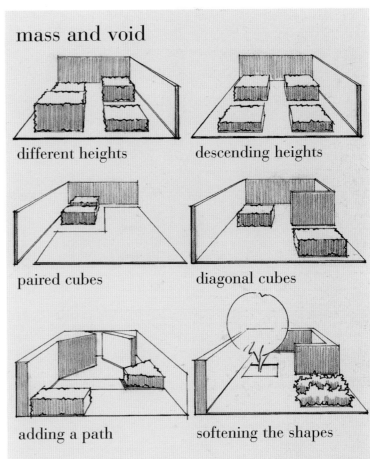

mass and void

different heights

descending heights

paired cubes

diagonal cubes

adding a path

softening the shapes

By moving planting masses around and changing their heights, you can alter the feel of a garden. The size of the masses will originally have come from your grid – but you can move them off the grid – it doesn't alter their proportion, and you can twist them as well. Thinking this way in terms of masses and the spaces between, you are starting to realize the garden design in three dimensions.

Some of the most interesting small formal garden layouts from the middle of the twentieth century have been constructed in Holland: formal, perhaps, though not necessarily traditional. A pioneer designer was the late Mien Ruys, (1908-1998), who drew ideas from other Dutch Modernists while also acknowledging a debt to the British plantsmanship of Robinson and Jekyll. Her lasting memorial is a series of small demonstration gardens at Dedemvaart in which she combined a formalized, directional design with a lush planting contrast.

Another Dutch designer working in the Mien Ruys tradition is Arend Jan van de Horst. He extended the idea of the formal garden, on a small, typically Dutch scale, using abstract plans often with masses of box. The photograph of Mien Ruys' garden and the illustration (see page 102) explain about volumes in a garden – often loosely filled with soft perennial shrubs or grasses, but with box masses becoming quite a strict exercise in height and scale. Hedges, of course, come into their own in Holland, providing wind shelter in this exposed land. Some of the most

softening the directionals

TOP A formal pattern of box-edged beds is infilled with soft flowering perennials and shrubby material. The fluffy cream flowering shrub is a species of sorbaria. This type of pattern might be called "slowed-down directional."

RIGHT A more strongly directional avenue planting of hornbeam (*Carpinus* species) casts beautiful shadows on the lawned area beneath it. Sunlight and shadow often strengthen a garden's dramatic intention.

"When I start to use the areas outside the pattern as well, the concept becomes even more dynamic".

exciting work today is practiced by the designer Jacques Wirtz, who works with his sons from their nursery in Belgium. Wirtz's designs are strongly directional, using the technique of pleaching of linden or hornbeam (a form of espalier, training the trees to grow laterally), and hedging, but also using underplanting in a very wild way to create an original yet formal look – the primary directional flow is slowed down by an underlayer of horticultural interest.

But how do these design influences affect the rest of us, wanting to lay out our garden and get on with its planting? What other designers' work does is to show us alternatives.

Moving elements around within a perimeter delineates movement. The elements could be trees, clumps of evergreen or lavender, even flowerbeds. When I start to use the areas outside the pattern as well, the concept becomes even more dynamic. It is not only the pattern that is important – it is what is left over, but within the perimeters. At this point you move from linear direction toward movement in shape.

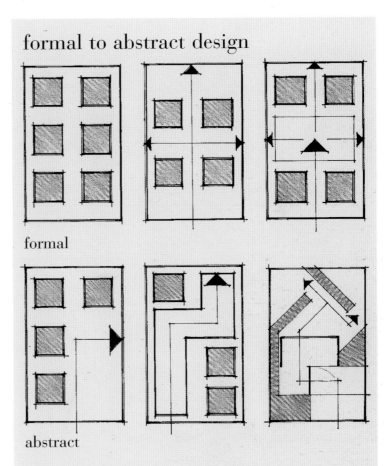

formal to abstract design

formal

abstract

Six diagrams illustrate how the designer can move from a formal design based upon symmetry to one of asymmetric formality. It is an exercise in manipulating space, according to site. The final drawing has moved the concept through to abstraction. All these designs evolve from a basic grid or module. The spaces between the shaded blocks of planting become pathways.

abstracted layout

In this town garden by Arend Jan van der Horst, the formal pattern has been slightly abstracted in that the flowerbeds do not line up. This creates a much less obvious directional feel to the garden, although I would still call it a formalized concept, which would be ideal for a small garden or for an area of terrace within a larger "sub-urban" or country layout. Topiary is once again introduced to punctuate garden plantings.

slow, indirect paths

A natural garden calls for paths, whether hard or soft, to allow the user to wander and make discoveries, so that all is not revealed at first glance. An indirect path helps to slow down one's progress through a garden, whether large or small – and allows the user to pause and discover new areas or corners. To create an indirect route through a design, use planting masses at intervals to interrupt the route, or create a winding paved or mown strip through longer grass or meadow to add interest to the route.

access paths or areas

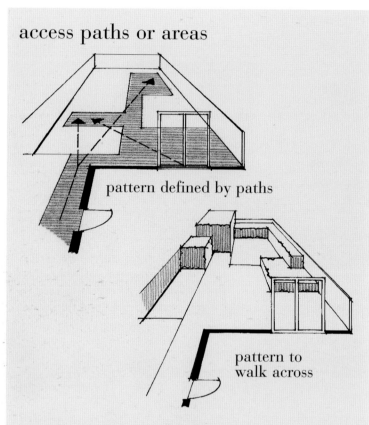

pattern defined by paths

pattern to
walk across

The dotted lines in the diagram (top) indicate the routes from a house, down
the side passage, and out through the sliding glass doors. The paths perhaps
lead to a log pile on the left and a terrace at the far end of the garden. The
areas of garden between the paths do not contribute much to the design – they
are leftovers. If you now abstract the same layout (above) and add some
planting, you can still walk across large areas of paving, but you are looking
into a total outside-room concept, rather than a space defined by footpaths.

pattern of decking

This abstracted pattern for an exhibition show garden
was conceived as a series of decking squares, some of
which were built up to provide seating and a plinth for
planted containers. Another square was placed on end
to provide an instant screen from the neighbors. A
further square beyond provides another terrace that
overlooks a natural pond. The scale of the planting
masses does not distract from the design. In fact, the
foliage color blends well with the pebble areas.

The overall shape becomes more important than the elements
from which it is made. This is one of garden design's really
important factors.

A two-dimensional balance can be upset by three-
dimensional volume. The height of the elements of the design
should reinforce your planned intention. And it is not only the
volumes of the masses, but the area of the voids between them –
the bits you walk on – which are important, too.

So this takes me to thinking about direction in terms of
function. There was a time when the routes within a garden,
from the house to the compost, from the compost to the tool
shed, and so on, were seen as what made the garden functional
– the avenues of grand gardens had been scaled down to
domestic proportions. The features were fine, but what about
the leftover bits? Increasingly, as we evolve gardens as
interlocking spaces, the hard surfaces of the old routes can
become part of larger areas of terrace or gravel. You can still walk
straight over them – but the route is not so directional.

"The overall shape becomes more important than the elements from which it is made. This is one of garden design's really important factors."

levels

*If your site is flat, try to create extra visual interest by introducing a change of
level. Just a single step running across the garden can make a huge difference.*

Perhaps some of the most difficult sites to design are those that
are completely flat. Their maintenance will be easy, but if the
layout is to be interesting, you need to find a way to hold the
eye so it does not run out of the site. In short, you need a focal
point – or two or three of them in progression – to create
internal interest as discussed in the previous chapter. You can
create "rooms" to break up a flat plot by simply changing the
character of various areas – a terrace, a checkerboard of planting
and paving, a lawn, some water, a gravel area, a herb garden,
and so on. Conversely, if the garden has external views – if it is
sited on flat land by the sea, among the fields of northern
France, even on the pampas of Argentina – allow some of the
character of that landscape to come into the site. That character
will most probably be defined by vegetation, though you might
interpret field patterns as well, as we have seen.

Flat areas may well be windy if there are few trees, and some
sort of shelter may be necessary. Try to use "wings" of plant
screen material, as on a stage, rather than surround the whole
garden with a hedge. This way you keep the view as well as
filtering the wind rather than blocking it on a windswept site.

In some locations, the scale of a flat open landscape can be
overwhelming, and you might well feel the need to frame it
with plant material to restrict the view. The garden will
naturally become a refuge. I personally find a broad sea view –
in Britain anyway – can be a bit depressing. Fine on a sparkling
sunny day – but depressing in winter. Again, this is where I
think a horizon broken by planting can add interest. For most
people, however, a big open view is not the problem – rather it
is how to create interest in a smaller, flat site.

Even a small step (as long as it is wide enough) running
across the garden can hold the eye and provide a visual check.
Add some water falling over it and you will double the effect,
since the play of light reinforces the intention. (I'll get to water
later.) If you include a step up, of course, you will need to have
one step down, if the site is really flat, but very few garden sites
are quite that featureless.

steps in small areas

Steps can become an architectural feature when used
to bridge the change in level from a raised upstairs
apartment down to a small town garden at ground
level. Here, open risers in this theatrical iron staircase
allow light to reach through to the shade-loving ferns
growing beneath the stairs. The spiky cordyline plant
in full light with its accompanying classical oil jar on
the wooden deck provide a good contrast to the ferns
and the dramatic change of level.

contouring the banks of a stream

Dramatic level changes in a large garden can be produced by earth shaping and contouring, as well as by introducing hard architectural structures, such as steps and ramps to the site. Here, a stream (whose source lies in the hilly landscape beyond the boundary of the garden) runs through a downland garden, and has been dammed at intervals to create a series of natural-looking ponds (top sketch) which look like they have always been a part of the setting. The excavation of the ponds, with a hired digger, produced surplus soil, which was used elsewhere in the site (although, if you do not have the space you may have to remove the soil from the site altogether which can be expensive). The banks at the water's edge were then gently graded in an attempt to imitate the soft contours of the surrounding landscape. Ideally, the angle of the banks should not be more than 45° to the horizontal, to aid mowing and general maintenance of the grass.

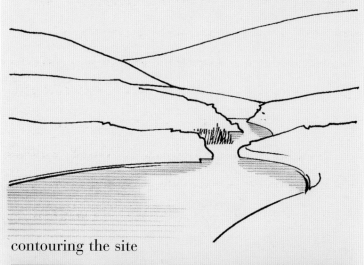

contouring the site

the finished pond

"...think about some gentle contouring to break up the flatness of your site."

Imagine that you are going to have a swimming pool dug in your garden, and you are told you will save a considerable amount of money if you retain the excavated earth for the pool in the garden rather than carting it away. How would you use it? To screen a nasty view, or to block the sound from the road?

Highway noise, particularly if the road is concrete, can travel a considerable distance. An earth bank is the most effective way to muffle it – much better than planting (though you can use planting in addition).

However, even if you are not planning on building a swimming pool (and some would say "how wise"), think about some gentle contouring to break up a flat site. One small machine (many are now small enough to get onto site via a narrow entrance) working for a day can create an undulation of as little as 3 ft (1 m) high with which you can work. Where you have gone up, you will have created a bowl – how about a water garden? Since water runs downhill, you will create a damp area anyway, unless you have very porous ground. So use this to

earth shaping

In this well-conceived front garden at a beach-house location in Uruguay, South America, the grassed-over lawn area on each side of the garage entrance has been earth-shaped to echo the contours of the sand dunes which can be seen across the road (the sea is on the horizon beyond them). The arrangement of native plant material in gently curving beds and the proportion of the plants, match the scale and roll of the contoured lawn areas. The cultivated plants also echo the appearance of the plants growing on the sand dunes beyond the garden.

create a feature. On the contoured area you can plant or grass over, but you will have created internal interest.

Still on the subject of level changes, increasingly raised beds are being used to either grow vegetables – this way you can enrich quite small areas for cultivation – or to give planting added height. Treated wood is used to create a simple formal effect, and this can be extended so the beds become decorative as well. Such an elevation creates instant interest since it places you in the garden rather than on it. You are back to that early medieval grid pattern.

If you accept the idea of a garden being a collage of shapes, stepping those shapes on a site that is not flat makes the whole concept take on a new meaning, since there can then be a separation between each "room" in the form of a step or steps. This is not the sort of space that will necessarily be suitable for children with wheeled toys; instead it becomes a "strolling" garden.

In the diagram below, I have shown an example of working the other way, that is, by sinking the garden, but, even so, unless you dispose of the excavated soil from the site, you still need to find a way to reuse it.

sunken gravel garden

Lowering the ground level of an area of your garden to create a sunken garden can be a great eyecatcher. This sketch outlines the plan for an English-style sunken garden I designed for a Japanese garden show in Osaka. The retaining walls are of reconstituted stone with brick capping. Excavated materials went into the raised and retained planted area behind. In the center is a gravel area with fountains, and soft meadowlike planting surrounds the fountain basins. The effect was both pretty and stunningly different for the visitors.

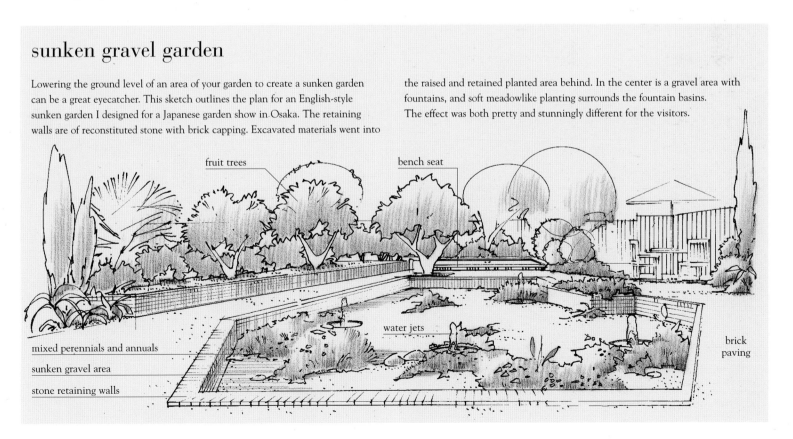

fruit trees

bench seat

mixed perennials and annuals

sunken gravel area

stone retaining walls

water jets

brick paving

contouring

It is probably only on larger sites that you can contemplate contouring to any significant extent, but if you are excavating for a pool and can use the spoil on site, you will save money. There are two approaches to earth. Creating a crisp, chiseled finish is one way – though it is difficult to maintain, the effect can be spectacular. Or you can aim to create more rolling contours. These should fit into the landscape, and not appear to be a "dump" of earth upon it. When contouring the landscape you should always work with subsoil. Keep the topsoil separate and reserve it to use for the final soil covering before planting up the area.

> *"If you accept the idea of a garden being a collage of shapes, stepping those shapes on a site which is not flat makes the whole concept take on a new meaning..."*

level changes

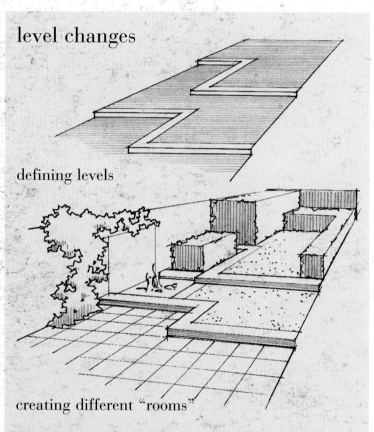

defining levels

creating different "rooms"

In a small garden with subtle changes in level, use a series of wide steps stretching across the site to define the different areas. Even in a small, flat garden site, you can create interest with just two level changes – a step down to a lower level and a step up to a raised level. In this example, the steps could be made of wood, brick, concrete, or stone – it doesn't matter. Use different materials to distinguish the levels – a paved lower terrace, a central gravel area, and a lawn on the top level with blocked in areas of vegetation.

This arrangement of levels may flow up from the house (watch the drainage) or down from it to a view out of the site or to the end of the garden. But the level surrounding the house will be the point from which you work out into your other levels. The grid still works – but of course you will make your pattern work with what you know of your site and connect, with a step or steps, the different levels. This transition from house through terrace and into garden is very important and, I believe, should all be part of one architectural concept. It can be a South London town garden, or a northern country garden, somewhere in Canada or in Timbuktu, it does not matter. Steps are for the convenience of the people who use them. They are the common denominator, interpreted through the right building materials for the particular location. Steps either up or down, which are turned to run parallel with the house (or terrace) take up less space and allow you to approach the garden at an angle should your layout be asymmetric. When working with a site that is not level, make sure the terrace is right first. The terrace is the

levels from the house

The entrance to this seventeenth-century manor house had very narrow steps to the front door. They were surfaced with knapped or cut flint, and edged with brick. This technique is quite particular to areas of chalk where flints occur naturally. (Knapped, or cut, the inside of the flint looks like marble.) The steps were extended in the same material to provide a better plinth for the scale of the house, and allow plenty of room for pots of annuals and bulbs to sit upon them.

"The terrace is the plinth on which the house sits. In the same way that a base wrongly proportioned to a piece of sculpture will "kill" it, so a wrongly proportioned plinth unsettles the house."

plinth on which the house sits. In the same way that a base wrongly proportioned to a piece of sculpture will "kill" it, so a wrongly proportioned plinth unsettles the house. This will be true from all aspects, front and rear and on the sides, too. Very often, we make our plinth structures too narrow, so be generous. Of course, since the top terrace usually has a hard surface, to make the transition from inside to outside, it is cheaper if it is smaller. But it's a false economy. Use cheap materials if you like, but get that proportion right. There is no firm rule of thumb, but usually the width of a terrace should be the height to the first story – it is the height of your living room or kitchen, too – think about laying them flat if you pushed the wall down. Anything narrower becomes a path around the house, and does

not have generous enough proportions to be described as a terrace. Once this plinth for your house has been established, you are ready to take off up or down. "It is not always realized how much additional charm is given by the well conceived design of steps, and how great a variety lies open to the straying choice," wrote Miss Jekyll in *Gardens for Small County Houses*. She was right in her sentiment, but it now needs an update.

In many smaller gardens the problem is not necessarily "a flight" of steps. Instead, a broad change of level is appropriate, needing only one step or perhaps two. Even one or two steps though, need considering as part of the whole, for level changes are great eyecatchers and help to create ground level interest in a garden. This, of course, is something that will last the whole year, too – steps are part of the architecture of the place, and few plants can compete. Indeed, where steps, even one or two, lead from a terrace adjacent to the house, they are part of the architecture of the house as well. And here's the crunch – steps may be of the house, or they may be of the

calculating the size of the terrace

"How wide should a terrace area be?" is a question that I am frequently asked by design students. If the terrace area is for outdoor eating and relaxing, I think it should be the same dimensions as the first floor of the house. These dimensions will also visually balance the proportions of the house. It is always better to have a large terrace than one that is too small to serve a useful purpose.

the terrace as plinth

LEFT The steps up to the house and the generous terrace area have been made using wide cedar boards on a rigid platform. Light wooden furniture continues the simple cedar styling. Such a terrace supports the house upon it as well as providing a useful and convenient outside "room."

"...steps may be of the house, or they may be of the garden or countryside beyond. The degree of connection one way or the other will depend upon the size of the garden..."

garden or countryside beyond. The degree of connection one way or the other will depend upon the size of the garden and the scale of the level that has to be traversed.

It is not usually enough to duplicate the dimensions of indoor steps outside, for outdoor steps need a greater scale and their dimensions can be much more generous. Very broadly, the higher each step is, the faster one goes up them – and a garden, however large, isn't a place for rushing around. The materials you use to build your steps will to a degree dictate their dimension. Think about this one as you go up or down steps in public places or in other people's gardens. You will feel what a difference there can be and how much of Miss Jekyll's "charm" (as described on the previous page) is added by the right dimensions.

Some of the most important steps lead to the front door of a house. They are seen with the elevation of the house and are often part of a porch or front door detail. So take your clues to material choice and scale from the elevation of the house itself.

shallow steps

Bold cast-concrete steps, while matching the solidity of this concrete house and its retaining walls are, at the same time, both wide and shallow. They create an impressive entrance entirely in scale with the proportions of the building. The slate infill of the terrace and the matching ornamental blue china ball are stylish additions.

terraced garden design

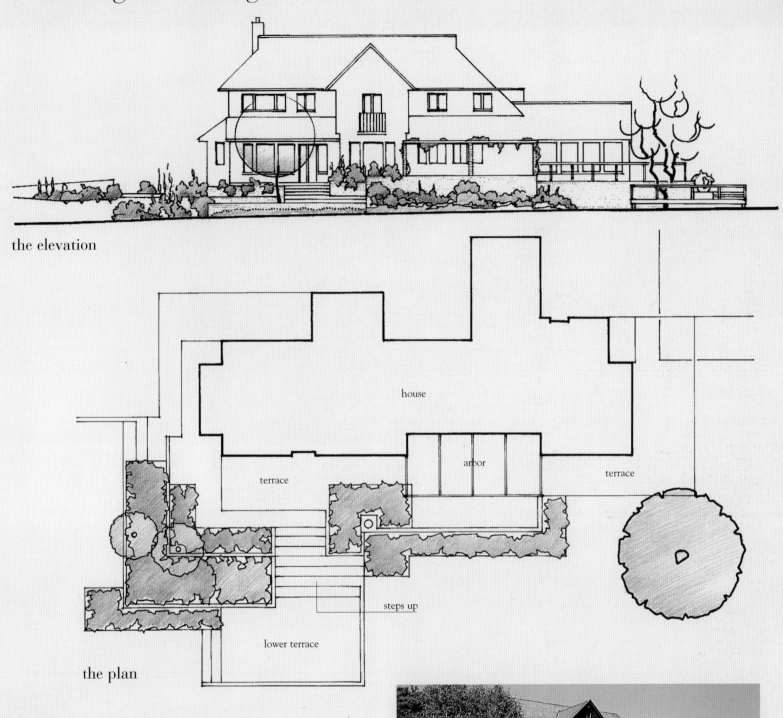

the elevation

the plan

house

arbor

terrace

terrace

steps up

lower terrace

This cedarwood house needed a plinth to fuse it and the garden to its site on a steep wooded hillside. The client wished to create a series of wide terraces on the south-facing facade for eating out and entertaining. The drawing of the elevation shows how the client's wishes were achieved. A brick retaining wall visually extends the house outward so it sits more happily upon a generous brick base. The plan shows the concept as mapped out, with terraces of concrete slabs and generous, wide steps connecting them. Four years after completion (right), the construction has mellowed, with shrubs and climbers softening the walls at different levels.

mature garden

steep, fast steps

A garden is not a place for rushing about in but a place for spending time out from your daily routine to relax. But sometimes, when you have to go up or down an incline or rapid change of level in a limited space in the garden, you need steep steps to move faster across the area. For example, entrance steps from the street level up to the front door of a townhouse may need to be steep.

Consider your choice of materials for steep steps as they can be more dangerous than other garden steps, and perhaps think about installing a handrail to make it easier and safer to climb up and down. Plant material on each side of steep steps will also soften what can be an imposing architectural entrance.

"Very broadly, the higher each step is, the faster one goes up them – and a garden, however large, isn't a place for rushing around."

The construction of steps should be very sound and certainly non-slip. Brick, tile, or wood inserts can cross stone or concrete paving to help give a grip on frosty or snowy mornings. Lighting is important, too, preferably across the step at ground level. Higher lighting casts a greater shadow, making the step look larger.

On the other side of the house, the step into the garden is the first level change. Make that step generous. It is so useful to put things on, to sit on, or to leave muddy boots. There is usually some paving and, where you have level problems, steps up or down to the remainder of the garden.

The classic flight of steps will be in the middle of the terrace with a balance on each side, and this may well set the pattern for the remainder of the garden layout. But I think we can learn much from period country house garden style by seeing how a twist in the steps or a change of direction can give the layout a whole new dimension. Lutyens inserted the odd rill or small pond with his – often quite small – flights of steps. Occasionally

allow a plinth on the steps for a large tub. Quite often, small step dimensions only allow space for small pots, so you need a lot of them and that means frequent watering. In rocky or arid regions of the world, boulders are often included within the stepped pattern, and they make a good punctuation in the horizontal line. The broader your horizons, the wider your steps may be.

Steps are constructed with treads (the bit you walk on) and risers (which give them height). The materials for each need not necessarily be the same. Keep your treads generous. I like treads that are 18 in (500 mm) wide and the riser to be between 3-8 in (80-170 mm). The scale of the area and the possibilities of different step materials make a set formula for the calculation of tread and riser very difficult.

As a general rule, treads should be wider than the average length of a foot, no less than 14 in (350 mm). To make sure that water is not retained upon the tread (making them slippery), create a fall of no less than 1 in (25 mm) on the side or forward, according to the design.

styles of garden steps

LEFT A balustraded staircase with statuary is in keeping with the character of this grand Italian villa.

TOP Curving brick steps create an elegant garden feature. The arc of the steps is repeated in the line of the wall, while the containers make another visual link.

ABOVE The terrace and wide steps use concrete slabs as the treads and brick for a retaining wall and step risers. The tread overhang of the riser is fairly large – it adds a "flying" elegance to a simple construction.

"Occasionally allow a plinth on the steps for a large tub – small step dimensions only allow space for small pots..."

Where slabs of stone or concrete form the tread, create an overhang of the tread over the riser of no less than ½ in (15 mm). The thickness of the tread will determine this dimension.

Steps in large gardens that are situated away from the house or which are located in a rural setting may be constructed as above, but they can also be made from railroad ties, lumber (preferably hardwood), or split planks. Any of these may be used to make both risers and treads, or can be mixed with chips or hoggin (an unwashed aggregate that includes clay as a binder).

Create generous landings of 3-6 ft (1-2 m) wide to break up long flights of steps. Try not to have more than ten or twelve steps between these landings, and where there is space, break up long flights of steps with gentle ramps instead of landings.

anatomy of a step

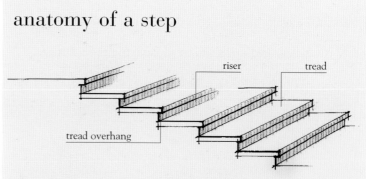

My preference is for wide step treads, 18 in (500 mm) wide, with a shallow riser of between 3-8 in (80-170 mm) – but these dimensions will depend upon the site and the space available for steps. A step flight with no overhang of tread becomes quite sharp and architectural. I prefer some overlap, dependent upon the material used in the construction. Where frost and ice is a hazard, make sure the steps are textured, allow for water to drain off, and provide both a handrail, particularly on an important approach, and ground-level lighting.

step details

LEFT These elegant steps incorporate the use of planted pots as a decorative detail. The pots mark the edge of the steps and soften the structure visually. The riser and the tread are brick and stone with a gravel backfill.

ABOVE This flight of Moorish-style steps has a rill down the middle, to allow a flow of water. The dark stone edging on each side contrasts with the pale limestone paving. It is this sort of detail that the architect Edwin Lutyens reinterpreted at Hestercombe.

Many people are unable to envisage what steps will look like – they can draw them on a plan in two dimensions, but come to a halt after that. By constructing a projection from your two-dimensional plan (see page 136), you will not only bring your plan to life, but also begin to see the other, smaller details that need resolving, such as what happens on either side of the steps, and what happens at the top and bottom of them as well.

Moving farther away from the house, you will see how your steps become part and parcel of the plinth that holds the house – the terrace, in fact – so they are inseparable from the house. They might still only extend over a slight change of level, but they may need to be widened against the scale of the house.

The same looser arrangement of stepped levels is often appropriate when looking away from the house, when the level change is seen as a feature against a garden backdrop or a wilder landscape outside the site. In mountainous or hilly areas, or by the ocean these step levels can be quite long and will be more rural in feel. And this is where wood comes into its own.

gradual level changes

TOP This gravel ramp has steps at wide intervals to make walking through a hilly woodland setting easier.

LEFT The scale of these sloping grassy steps is as magnificent as that of the mountains beyond. The steps have a rough stony surface, and a stone edging to improve drainage. On a smaller garden scale, substituting grass steps for low-growing thyme plants will release fragrance as you tread.

constructing a ramp

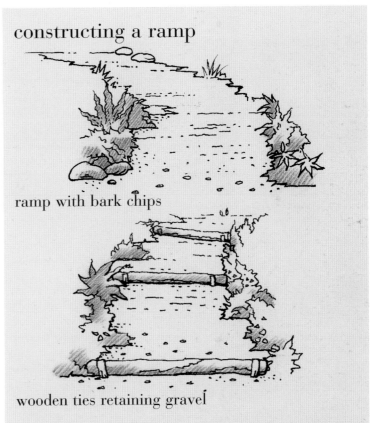

ramp with bark chips

wooden ties retaining gravel

As long as the gradient is not too steep, a ramp is much easier to negotiate than steps, particularly for wheeled maintenance vehicles – but you need space. In a woodland setting, use bark chips as an alternative to gravel – gravel, if not well consolidated, tends to run downhill. By introducing the occasional step, you inhibit this runoff of loose gravel, and you control the user's progression up or down the ramp as well. To anchor the wooden ties to their site, drive the tie into the bank at least 3 ft (1 m) on each side of the path.

shallow, slow steps

Gentle changes of level in a garden bring huge visual interest to it as well as introducing an immediate sense of direction and structure to the garden design. Shallow steps are appealing as they can act as an impromptu place to sit down and rest, or you can stand pots of annuals on their wide treads to bring added summer color to this architectural feature.

Even if you have limited space, be as generous as possible with the dimensions when designing steps. You will not regret it.

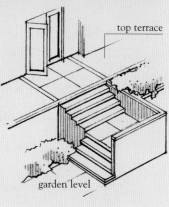

steps solutions

steps under construction

This steep step flight is under construction (above), and as yet has no handrail for safety. But as a structure, it offers a good solution for connecting the house to the garden level in what is obviously a difficult site with huge level changes. In the sketch (right), I have shown how low retaining brick walls could contain a step flight, and provide a sheltered terrace area along the way. Where appropriate, you could also construct a storage area in the space underneath the flight of steps.

top terrace

garden level

steep change of level

Consolidated gravel can be used to backfill the wooden timber risers of the steps, or you can consider ground-cover planting instead if they are not to take too much wear.

On any sort of flight of steps, you can break up their hardness by the introduction of plants – but make the masses obvious or they can become a hazard. And I would not use plants among steps that provide the main access to a house.

It is important that students of garden design understand how their levels will work – not only to clarify the concept in their own minds, but so that they can explain it to a prospective client, and eventually specify instructions to whoever will build the levels.

Contours seem to flummox people, since they are invisible. Most people are aware of contour lines (either close together or far apart) in terms of mountain ranges when they are looking at a school atlas – and, those who hike, of contours on detailed hiking maps. Garden landscape contours are more detailed, though in essence the same.

step materials

TOP This neat, small flight of steps would enhance any size garden. Using the same concrete slabs as the terrace for its treads, the brick risers and retaining walls are built using matching brickwork. Note that the treads are at least one-and-a-half bricks wide to make the step surface generous.

"By constructing a projection from your two-dimensional plan you will also begin to see the smaller details that need resolving, such as what happens on either side of the steps..."

It is important to realize that everywhere is between two contours (which are counted from sea level). If a site seems flat, the contours will be very far apart – on a gradient, the closer the contours, the steeper the bank.

Probably you will only use survey contours above sea level on a large site. As garden designers, we are normally only interested in levels up or down from a datum point – which you or the architect decide upon. If you are working with a structure, take datum or zero as the floor level of that structure.

You might be given levels from an architect's drawing of specifics existing on the site – trees, some steps, the garage. Or you might have to decide these levels yourself. They cannot be altered if they are a given. If you lack confidence, ask someone to determine levels for you – "spot levels" – at relevant places. You can indicate where you want levels taken on a plan, making an overlay with a grid and taking a level at each intersection. By joining up similar readings, you will establish your own contours at regular intervals.

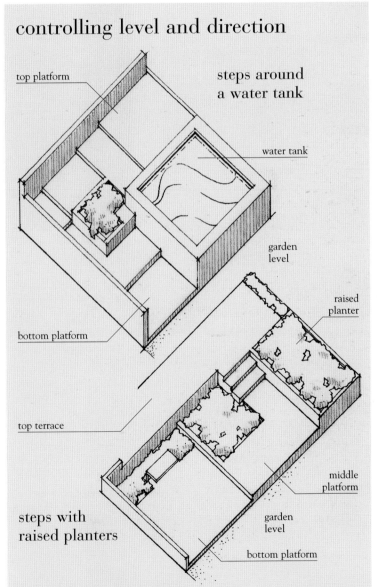

controlling level and direction

top platform

steps around a water tank

water tank

garden level

raised planter

bottom platform

top terrace

middle platform

steps with raised planters

garden level

bottom platform

These designs make the steps and change in levels into an attractive garden feature in their own right. They have been conceived as part of the initial garden design rather than as an afterthought. The first sketch (top) uses a series of shallow steps to move slowly down to the garden level, and these are worked in around a central water feature. This water tank will be the dominant feature, and the steps subsidiary. Below, steps are worked into broader level changes, where a series of sheltered platforms on different levels make these areas an attractive place to linger.

retaining walls between levels

Obviously the structure and materials of retaining walls determine how attractive they are, but the way you treat and plant the top or bottom of them is important as well.

In small gardens, as with steps, they make pleasant, casual places to sit. Where the walls are high, you can use hanging plants to soften the effect. If you are considering building a retaining wall more than 3 ft (1 m) high, you should seek expert advice, both about reinforcing the wall, and the possible drainage problems that may result from the build-up of heavy soil behind it.

"On any sort of flight of steps you can break up their hardness by the introduction of plant material..."

This concept is fairly easy to transfer to the computer screen if you have the correct program – it is this sort of task rather than as a design tool for which computers are perfect, I believe. So you now have a survey, with a structure and a series of horizontal lines sweeping about which are your contours.

As you evolve your design – remember that you have seen the site and know it – create a brief at the bottom (the "lollipop" diagram it is sometimes called) and mark a ring around the areas where it is sunny for sitting, where it is windy, what has a good or bad view, and so on. Over that you will place your grid taken from the house. Now impose the contours, and over that start to adjust them according to your design (see illustration page 142).

Remember contours are like flexible wires. You pull them apart to create a flat area; and the closer they are, you either create a bank, or if they are really close together, you may need a wall to retain them. Banks, incidentally, should not be more than 45° if they are to be stable. If they are to be grassed, mower manufacturers suggest that to maintain the banks, the angle

steps with plants

LEFT A short flight of wooden steps is well integrated into beautiful surrounding planting of grasses and perennials by Mein Ruys in Holland.

RIGHT Planting worked into the steps should only be used when the flight is not a main one, for their purpose is decorative, and very beautifully so in this case, but plants may be a hazard as well. Remember when laying the treads to your steps that water should run off, or they can become dangerous in bad weather.

building up your contour plan

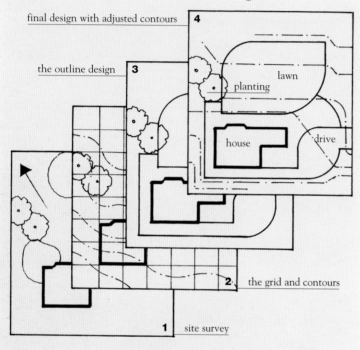

final design with adjusted contours **4**

the outline design **3**

lawn

planting

house   drive

2 the grid and contours

1 site survey

This sequence of drawings shows all the stages of planning a garden from the initial site survey. The student of garden design goes through this process with each drawing on tracing paper to achieve an accurate end result.

1 An accurate survey of your site.
2 The grid taken from the proportions of the house.
3 An outline design.
4 Temper this outline by including levels and contours.

should not be more than 30° from the horizontal for safety reasons and ease of maintenance.

To accompany the illustrated diagram (left), I would like to clarify the sequence of drawings when evolving a garden plan, which includes building up levels and contours.

The first drawing – at the bottom of the pile as it were – will be an accurate survey of the site on which you will delineate its key features, like a north point, prevailing wind direction, good and bad views, services, and, of course, existing trees and vegetation. On the second drawing you will evolve your grid taken from the proportions of the house. On the third drawing you start to evolve an outline design.

And finally, on the fourth drawing you temper this outline project by including levels and contours. If you have a huge contour change, that last plan might supersede the outline design. If you produce these four drawings on tracing paper and put them together, one on top of the other (see left), you will have every circumstance of your particular site at your fingertips.

contoured mounds

TOP I came across this contouring in a small park in Aix-en-Provence, France. I loved the shaping and the cypress planting, which related to the apartment buildings surrounding the area. Though steep, these mounds are still quite mowable, and they have a lovely organic flow to them. This is the secret – they do not look like the earth has just been dumped onto the site, but carefully and thoughtfully shaped.

planting shrubs on contoured land

This is a job I have been working on in central Chile – a new entrance drive to a courtyard house in the countryside. Huge eucalyptus trees shade the area, so the entrance drive has to work its way between the massive tree trunks. Surrounding the site is a private road which needed screening from the house since people using it could peer in. So contouring was introduced with planting over the top. Nothing grows under eucalyptus but eucalyptus – so the screen is of – you've guessed it – but cut down regularly. Within the site further contouring muffles the sound of cars on the drive from the house.

The stream had to be cleared (below left), and the photograph (below right) shows the driveway between eucalyptus trunks prior to the arrival of earth for contouring. As the stream flows only after excessive rain, we grassed over both it and the surrounding shaped ground with a shade-loving grass seed, and so far, I believe, it has been a success. Areas of shrub planting, beyond the shade of the eucalyptus trees, overlaid the contours to create screening formations in their own right, dividing up the separate functions of the site.

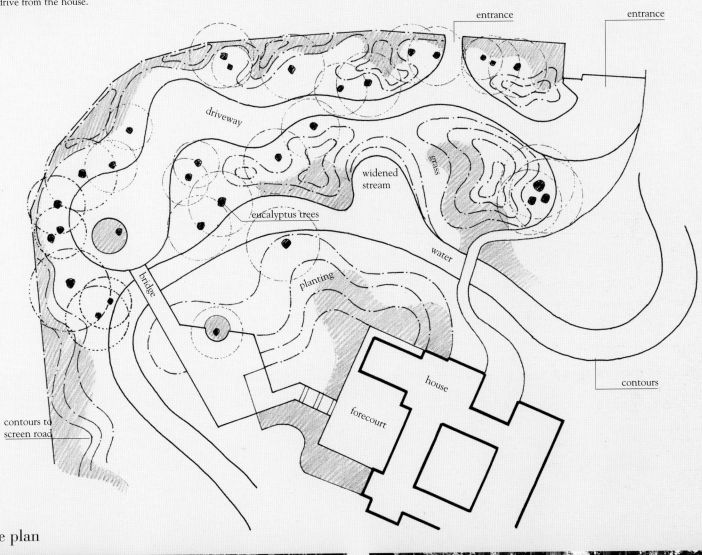

the plan

the stream

the driveway

proposed earth-shaping and planting

Traffic noise is a near-universal problem. This property has a busy road along its northern edge, and the landscape project was to introduce contouring with planting to conceal the road and cut down the noise level. Only solid earth really keeps out traffic noise – even thick evergreen planting only muffles it. But with the two together, I hope to have resolved the problem.

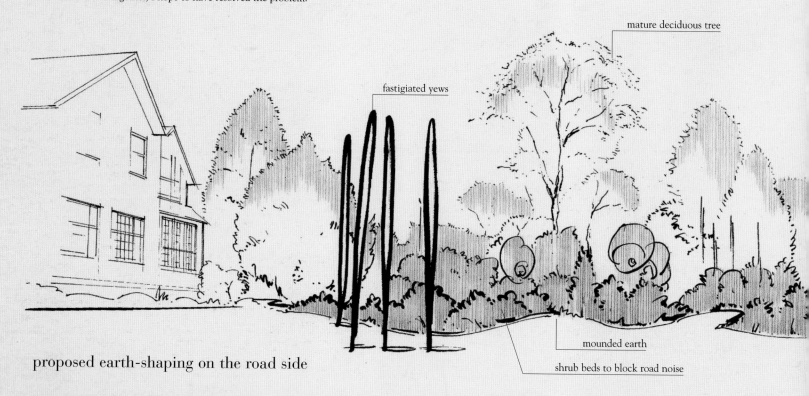

mature deciduous tree

fastigiated yews

mounded earth

shrub beds to block road noise

proposed earth-shaping on the road side

the level site prior to earth-shaping and planting

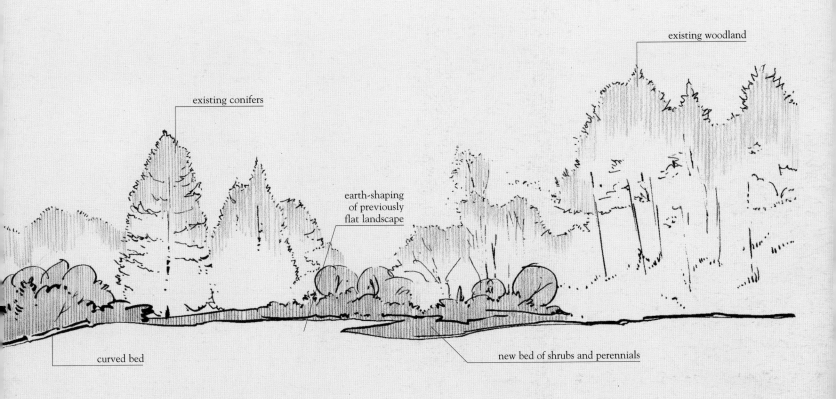

existing woodland

existing conifers

earth-shaping
of previously
flat landscape

curved bed

new bed of shrubs and perennials

enclosure

Enclosure is all to do with protection, safety, and marking your territory, while keeping the world at bay. Indeed, privacy is a major part of its purpose.

There is always a problem in evolving a book like this, in trying to decide the order of priority of the headings. Probably there is no correct priority – it is what happens to be appropriate and of interest to the reader at the time.

But there is something fairly important and "up front" about enclosure, which covers compounds, patios, paddocks, fields, parks, rings, courts, and no doubt many more. It is all to do with protection, safety, and marking your patch. All quite primitive aspects of privacy, in fact – or is that very British? What about all those open front yards in the United States?

Actually, as gardens get smaller, more fences are going up in the U.S. – since many of the houses now take up 75 percent of their lot, and privacy becomes increasingly important. In fact, it is probably less to do with protection and preventing people from coming in (although this is more relevant to inner-city life), and more about stopping children and dogs from getting out.

But beyond this, the privacy of your garden – if you choose to make it attractive enough – can be very special. It is amazing how invasive just one neighboring window overlooking your garden or one small view into it can be.

So enclosure is all about keeping the world at bay. And in the country surely one needs to see the view, block the wind, keep out the deer or rabbits and, in Australia, the kangaroos. We all have our problems.

Fortunately, enclosure is not only concerned with putting up walls and fences or planting hedges on the perimeter of the site; it is about masking the view as well, so that some element of surprise is introduced.

I think my first real awareness of not privacy, rather the enclosure that leads to the feeling of it, was within the courtyards of the Alhambra in Granada, Spain.

The heat, the fragrance of wisteria and citrus, the echo of water were all intensified in these gardens before the arrival of the daily throng. There was a time when, from the neighboring parador, you could get into the garden in the early morning – and it was magical. All the images which Washington Irving in

sheltered enclosure

This walled enclosure to a California home serves a dual purpose. It welcomes visitors (almost embraces them, in fact) and with a wide curve of steps creates a sculptural feature that further enhances a single olive tree. It is a simple statement but makes a very handsome architectural feature. The curved wall structure is of cast concrete that has been painted white and therefore matches the steps, which are made of the same material.

"Decide whether you want a view out of the enclosure, or whether you definitely wish to hold the eye within the area."

perimeter enclosure

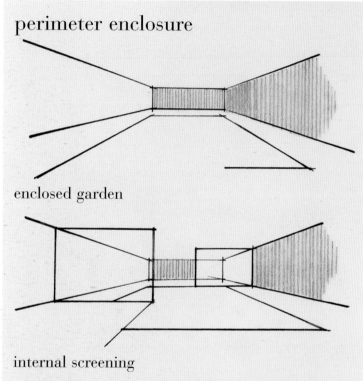

enclosed garden

internal screening

Walls that are constructed solely as a perimeter enclosure, to keep intruders out and children and dogs in, can be restricting and intimidating in appearance. Planting a screen of shrubs and trees and planning a well-conceived internal ground pattern of screens can alter this. By designing a series of internal screens, you create more garden interest and add a touch of mystery to the overall plan as you never know quite what lies beyond. Internal screens do not have to be walls as such. They can be made of hedging, or loose shrub material. You can create a similar effect with trees. Internal screens also serve as useful baffles for hiding storage units, trash cans, compost bins, play spaces, and the like.

his *Tales of the Alhambra* described in the nineteenth century came to mind – the rosé and the nightingale, and so on. So much in Spanish music encapsulates the romance and moodiness of these Moorish outside rooms – and that is another thing: you are never sure where inside ends and outside begins. Water runs both in and out of buildings and pavilions to cool the air, and the lush marble floorings are continuous.

Now I am not suggesting that anyone can recreate such a paradise, but there is a lot to be learned from experiencing this phenomenon.

First of all, to be really enclosed you need a fence higher than 5ft 6in (1.75 m). There is no substitute for a walled enclosure. Add greenery to a fence or wall and they instantly become comfortable rather than imprisoning. Bring in a tree to give a partial overhead canopy, and you begin to create a wraparound effect.

Decide whether you want a view out of the enclosure, or whether you definitely wish to hold the eye within the area.

privacy and coolness

TOP A narrow view between stone walls at the Fondation Maeght sculpture gallery, St. Paul de Vence, France – a series of walled enclosures.
RIGHT This fourteenth-century Moorish garden has a central Visigothic (pre-Islamic) fountain that feeds into rills, creating a true quartered garden. The rills run into the buildings to cool them. Carpets would have been placed around the rill, for people to sit on and enjoy the cool and contemplative atmosphere.

courtyard gardens

There is something about courtyard enclosures that is most attractive. It is probably the intimate scale of this external room that we relate to. In town the courtyard is often your garden, your outside room, even your car–parking area. With more space a courtyard becomes an interesting corner between buildings, and for those with avant-garde leanings it can become the central core of an atrium-style house.

inside out

A small area of garden like a roof garden, terrace, or balcony, particularly when located in town, becomes much more of a furnished room outside than a garden. If the space is sheltered, all it may need is a table and chairs, lighting (for eating outside in the evening), and possibly a water feature to help create a cool atmosphere in summer. There isn't necessarily much room for plants. On the other hand, with adequate maintenance, you can create a little plant jungle, but at the cost of space.

"...you could sink a portion of the garden to create a central focus. Paving might do it – a water feature certainly will, as will statuary, sculpture, even topiary. Make your statement bold."

a sunken enclosure

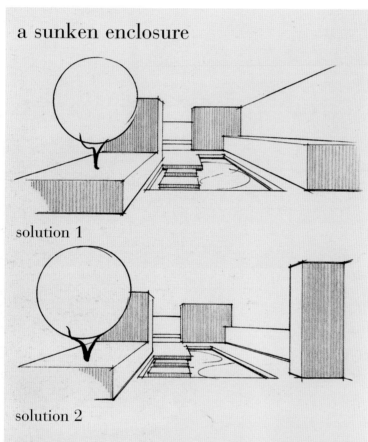

solution 1

solution 2

In the sketches above I have suggested a pool with stepping stones through it (top) to create a central interest and hold the eye in an enclosed garden. The addition of height in the foreground (above) helps to direct the eye down the site. I have shown the planting as block masses, which could equally well be colorful, and the water could have planting in it, too. The basic layout should read more strongly than its horticultural decoration.

If the latter, you could sink a portion of the garden to create a central focus. Paving might do it – a water feature certainly will, as will statuary, sculpture, even topiary. Make your statement bold. Remember that "little" is out – and "cute" even more so.

If you want to break a sense of complete enclosure with a view, use your design to direct the eye where you want it to go. Substantiate this with planting, which can be directional as we have seen, or more simply by marking the opening with two tall trees, not necessarily opposite each other. You can use different heights of tree and stagger their positioning, framing your intended view. Then, while still being enclosed you can break an overall view of your garden with "wings" of planting coming in from the side, partially blocking the total effect. These "wings" could also act as a frame to what is beyond, and create an air of mystery. The lines can be formalized or flowing, depending upon your style. In a roof garden in Japan, for instance, I used lattice pierced by arches to break up the wind-blown space into individual "English garden" rooms.

sheltered roof garden

A roof garden needs high enclosing walls to protect it from the constant scourge of wind, which dries out the plants. Plants on a roof terrace, whether protected by an enclosure or not, need to be able to withstand drought. Small-leafed, gray-foliaged, or succulent plants are all suitable, anything in fact that is adapted to drought conditions. If irrigation is available, you can alter your plant selection, though adequate drainage and constant feeding then becomes a priority.

framing the view

Sometimes a whole garden can be directed toward the view. Or you can present it as a series of framed vignettes as you wander through. But too wide a view can be visually disturbing – it may also mean that the garden will lack shelter and be exposed to the elements.

Most gardens are directed toward a sitting place, a good plant combination, or a piece of traditional or modern sculpture. You as the designer must create your own views or focal points within the garden.

"On a roof garden in Japan... I used lattice pierced by arches to break up the wind-blown space into individual "English garden" rooms."

Undoubtedly, what stops many people from creating a more structured boundary is the cost. But I think you can mix and match – having only a small piece of walling where it would be most crucial, with perhaps chainlink around the rest of the space through which ivy or vines may be grown.

There are many different types of enclosure. Many people do not have a choice because it comes with the property, and to change would cause neighbor problems. So work with what you have, and decide what you are trying to achieve. Chainlink with massed evergreens in front is a popular choice. The term evergreen sets some people's teeth on edge, and the urban look achieved with laurel, rhododendron, and conifer can be rather dead-looking. Add some evergold and evergray shrubs to it, and some different shapes, and you can liven it up considerably. It is to fulfill this screening objective that you can consider the use of climbers or vines. The number which are evergreen, however, is limited. The whole family of ivy (*Hedera* species) are very useful for these locations.

open, lightweight fencing

Many people would love to have a walled garden – it sounds so romantic apart from anything else – but the cost of construction is prohibitive. Lattice can be a good substitute for hard walls, especially when it is covered with vines or climbers. Also, for a roof terrace, where weight may be problem, lattice is ideal. Well-constructed lattice (even chainlink with climbers) is not as great a hazard as a solid structure because it filters the wind.

designing an enclosed roof garden

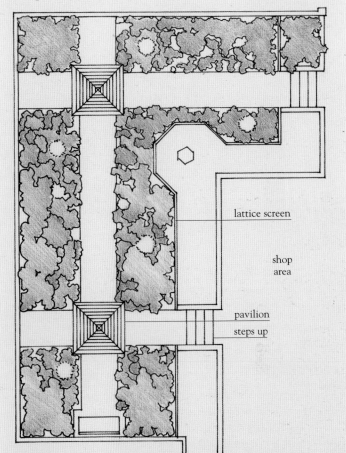

lattice screen

shop area

pavilion

steps up

the plan

the garden realized

The client brief for this rooftop enclosure in Kobe, Japan, was an enclosed English-style garden. There was adequate depth allowed in the roof surface construction for the growth of plants in the ground (with excellent drainage), but summer shade was vital, too. Enclosure was provided by structural walls, and the internal screening of lattice pavilions offered cool shade and support for climbers. The sunlight and humidity in this region in summer can be overwhelming, so the pavilions offer much-needed shade. Seats are placed at the end of pathways, to emphasize the directional axes, while a shop supplying garden plants and equipment occupies the adjacent site.

roof terraces

There is a simple pleasure to be had from being up at roof level surrounded by plants. But plants for exposed rooftop sites, often in full sun or buffeted by the wind, need to be selected with care or they will not thrive. Rooftop plants are often grown in containers (unless your building was constructed to hold the weight of a roof garden and its wet earth), and their root system is often limited. They require regular watering to prevent them from drying out. You should therefore choose your plants accordingly – what will grow on a mountainside will usually do well in a exposed rooftop location.

Alternatively, plan your rooftop as a plant-free outside room, with coloured walls for shelter, and cushions. Construct a space for storing furniture to save time and energy getting things in and out of the house.

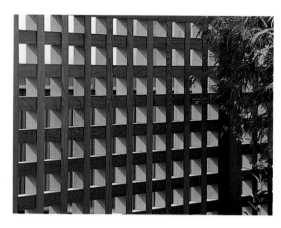

Chainlink and even wire mesh can serve a purpose, too. It can provide the necessary height to keep out deer and kangaroos. Just 3 ft (1 m), with the same amount buried beneath the ground deters rabbits, but you will also need self-locking gates where your boundary is broken by an entrance.

Between the open and enclosed boundary marker, there are endless fencing types. Many are built locally of local material – this is the true vernacular idiom, and I would go along with it where it is appropriate. Don't get too chic in a rural area or too urban in a country one, and bear in mind that your boundaries must work with your house style as well as their setting.

A new garden often needs enclosing, not only for privacy and screening, but for wind shelter as well. Indeed, if you live on a hill or near the sea, until you have established this enclosure there is little purpose in doing much else. But too often, in a haste to create shelter fast, trees or hedges are planted which first of all do not stop when they reach the required height, and second, need to establish a firm root run before they can take a

fencing materials

TOP In many cases a sturdy wooden grille is preferable to lattice, since the lifespan of softwood lattice is generally very short, particularly when it is covered by fast-growing climbing plants such as Russian vine (*Polygonum baldschuanicum*) or wisteria.
ABOVE The starkness of this wall has been broken by creating a horizontal banding of bamboo against it. It is a Japanese idea, complete with moss and maple, but is suitable for use almost anywhere.

> *"A new garden often needs enclosing not only for privacy and screening, but for wind shelter as well."*

buffeting. Fast growers on top tend to produce roots slowly. If you are trying to create an enclosure from wind, mix your planting.

Perhaps it is appropriate at this stage to give a warning about the planting of leylandii (*Cupressocyparis leylandii*) as an enclosure. They grow to 60 ft (20 m) in height very quickly. While their rate of growth might seem desirable on a new windswept site, or to give privacy around an urban one, you will quickly regret your choice when you find yourself looking at an unchanging green barrier from an upstairs window. And in the close proximity of an adjoining property, your neighbors will as well – which they may not always appreciate!

You can, of course, chop the top of the hedge off – but it will grow again, and get thicker, too. After a while, some of the trees will die for lack of nutrients due to competition at root level – but these deaths will not be in a regular pattern and you will have created a very raggedy effect. Despite these reservations, an occasional leylandii can be a worthy addition to your garden, though they do tend to be shallow rooted.

enclosed town garden

screen planting
compost
terrace
pond
lawn
screen planting
steps up
eating out
bar
log pile

the plan

This plan of a small town garden uses all the tricks of the trade both to provide privacy and to create internal interest. The garden already had a 4 ft 6 in (1.5 m) high wall. Thick planting was used to soften it and to create internal pockets of interest, such as a wall fountain and a private corner area for sunbathing. An additional stretch of wall runs from the house to create an outside dining room with steps down to the garden below. A central lawned area has a pool to one side, linked visually to the wall fountain, and on the far side of the lawn, a pavilion screens the compost area behind. Half the lawn has a paved border; the remainder is surfaced with loose gravel. Both surfaces allow plants the freedom to grow without being contained by rigid boundaries, and need not be cut back prior to mowing. The basic design is evolved on the square, since the site is so regular. Sheltered and enclosed urban gardens in Britain have a microclimate, and with good drainage all sorts of plants can be grown – even those not usually associated with an area.

screens for shelter

Seaside gardeners will know that without shelter from the elements, nothing grows. The same applies to any windy garden, like a rooftop garden, for example. In these locations, wind shelter has to be a primary consideration. Your screen can be a solid-built structure, or it may be created by planting up shrubs or trees. In the latter case, you need to establish the screen before planting the area within.

sheltering a coastal garden

This house faces south west toward an estuary and into the prevailing wind. The garden has to provide enclosure and/or screening from the wind while not blocking the view. The front access to the house, (left of plan) has been screened by a wall covered with an arbor. This area provides shelter at the windiest times. Plant material that grows in such an exposed place is fairly limited since the wind is extremely salt-laden. Beyond the planting for shelter is a meadow garden, which thrives in the brilliant light reflected off the water.

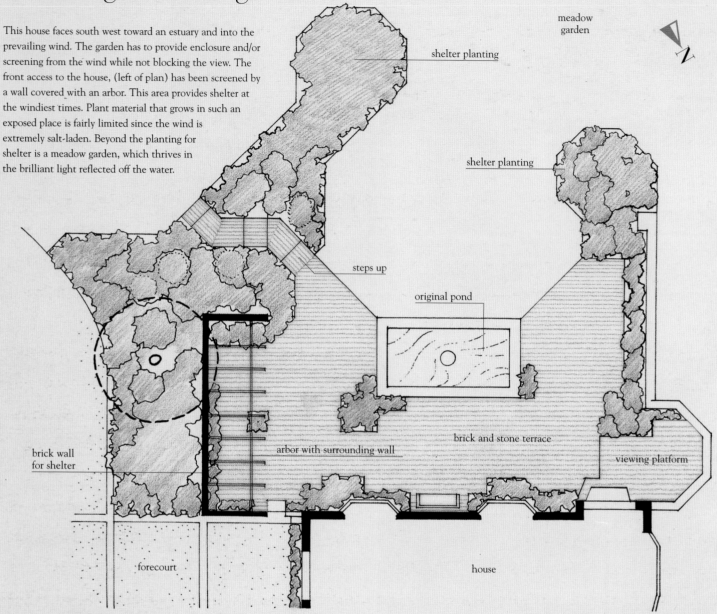

meadow garden

shelter planting

shelter planting

steps up

original pond

brick and stone terrace

viewing platform

arbor with surrounding wall

brick wall for shelter

forecourt

house

plan of the coastal garden

the pond and planting with meadow beyond

the house, the pool, and estuary behind

"...if you live on a hill or near the sea, until you have established this enclosure there is little purpose in doing much else."

As we will see, I think that there are many better ways of creating a growing enclosure.

We used to opt for a surrounding hedge to give us privacy within a garden, but a tree will do the trick just as well and has the advantage of needing much less maintenance than a hedge. Then beneath the occasional tree, you can create a loose background of evergreen shrubs as a substitute for the cover of the hedge.

Another option was to plant the trees on the boundary, leaving a great open central space to be expensively mowed and cared for and with half the tree's beauty in the garden next door – and the likelihood of complaints about whose right it is to cut it. Now that we are considering the garden more as an overall pattern, trees can come into the center of the garden and will do a far better screening job – the nearer they are placed to the viewer, the better the job they do. The plants that grow in their shade have much more shape and form (as well as color in the main) than the sun-loving perennials – which in any case can

be seen through the stems and trunks of the trees. These trees need not, of course, be enormous when mature. I can think of little more beautiful than the common apple tree for instance – a multi-stemmed bush tree that provides spring blossom, later apples, and even mistletoe in winter.

Those living in Mediterranean climates might use the olive in a similar way. In the U.S. varieties of the smaller conifers can perform the same job – you can achieve quite quickly the effect of a house within an orchard planting. You select the ultimate size of tree, and you select the density of its head. Silver birch and forms of robinia have feathery foliage that provides screening but does not block out the light. It is worth buying semi-mature trees to give you instant shelter, or failing that, well-grown nursery stock. Much will depend upon access (tree roots are large and heavy), availability, and price. Just the right tree or two in the right place can make all the difference to a small garden – and by buying large, you may save years of waiting time and create instant privacy and/or enclosure.

closed fencing

This term refers to fencing that you cannot see through to the other side, and includes walling. There are many different examples of fencing and walling styles and materials in vernacular architecture around the world.

Solid fencing panels are widely used, and they are available in a variety of heights and sizes. Usually made of wood, they may be layered or woven. Traditional woven hazel panels give a rural feel, but as they were originally intended as temporary fencing during the lambing season, they do not wear well in the garden.

open fencing

This is the most common type of fencing and is usually built of wood or made of metal. Originally it needed to be livestock-proof, but now it often only delineates a site boundary. In gardens with vermin problems, you may need to net the lower half of the fence, and bury some netting underground so that vermin will not dig underneath.

entrance

Property entrances for pedestrian or car use can range from the small urban to the grand rural sweep. All require careful planning for day and night access.

The entrance to a front garden often sets the mood of the whole house and helps to create the all-important first impression. The entrance can be quite neat and urban and designed for people on foot, or it can be a sweeping drive. Between these extremes there are a million permutations – all hopefully getting you to the front door. A porch is very useful to provide shade when it is hot, and to keep out the rain in inclement weather, allowing you to ring the bell and wait to be heard without getting soaking wet or too hot.

The other sort of entrance to a garden is from the house on its private side. I believe we pay far more attention to this entrance than to the approach entrance. It is seen more often and in a more leisurely way, through sliding doors or at the end of a hall and so on. The garden is often enjoyed through this entrance at sitting height as well, and we lavish much attention on the terrace, which makes the transition from house to garden. At the front of the house, it is the porch that provides the transition from inside to outside (in carriage days, it was the

porte-cochère). At the garden side of the house, there are all sorts of structural transitions – the arbor (see pages 240-245), the loggia (see pages 236-239), and the conservatory (see pages 224-235).

There is also, in most houses, what used to be called the service entrance, now just the back door. Often dark and windswept with narrow access, this entrance may get the most day-to-day use, possibly for deliveries or as the quickest way to the garage, or by children with dirty shoes and dogs with wet paws. Where possible the drive should serve this entrance, so you can use it to unload your shopping.

We are becoming much more practical now. Our entrances and exits should reflect our modern lifestyles and serve the daily workings of the household.

I spend a lot of my time visiting different houses and often make my way through the enclosure of their gardens, so I am very well aware of whether my arrival is catered for or not. Can I make a plea for a highly visible number in an urban situation,

pedestrian entrance
I like the style of this urban entrance – the paintwork on the door, the window, and the metal frame supporting the pleached tree, which provides a neat, high hedge from the street, and privacy upstairs inside the house. The strong architectural forms in the building have been repeated in the foliage forms, particularly the varieties of Hosta species in the foreground. A tall iris (left) provides suitable contrast.

path to the front door

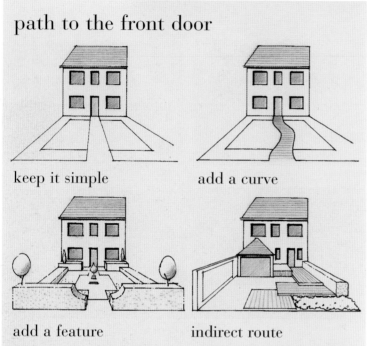

keep it simple   add a curve

add a feature   indirect route

Above are four alternative layouts for a front yard. The two layouts (top) are fairly conservative in their planning, with planting pushed to the boundaries. The first drawing shows a straight path direct to the front door, which repeats the geometry of the overall layout. The curved entrance path in the second drawing does not add anything and creates irregular lawn shapes, which do not fit into the geometry of the site. The bottom left suggestion has gone slightly over the top in its decorative treatment. What is suitable depends upon location. The fourth proposal has the addition of a garage. There is no reason why large parking areas need to be made of a uniform surface material – you can create a hard-surfaced pattern using different materials and introduce some minimal planting, which can be attractive.

and an obvious gateway or sign in a rural one? At night, can that sign be lit up as well? If I am driving, I need to know as soon as possible where to turn left or right – so the number or name on the house is not enough, if the approach road is some distance from the house. I can't both drive and peer into every gateway – obvious, really.

If I'm walking, I want to enter the site and think – "this is attractive," and be clearly routed to a front door as directly as possible. In *On the Making of Gardens* Sir George Sitwell sums it up by saying: "Curving paths cannot be right, for the Chinese themselves, with whom the landscape style began, make their paths straight, arguing that they must be due either to design or repeated passage, that no sober man will deliberately propose to reach his destination by a series of curves."

This doesn't mean to say that the path outline has to be straight; just your route across the paving. You are welcoming people in, so the route should be generous, the surface non-slip, and level changes lit. If the path is curving, let it be for a reason.

front door entrance

RIGHT A wide stone path welcomes you to the front door of this glass-fronted house. Running parallel with the house is a canal, which is crossed by a paved bridge, beneath the sliding entrance doors.
TOP Mark your house number as clearly as possible, and train a light upon it for night-time visibility, too. The larger the numerals used, the easier it is to see from a distance, which is important when traveling along a road by car.

"You are welcoming people in, so the route should be generous, the surface non-slip, and level changes lit. If the path is curving, let it be for a reason."

house entrance

Entrances should set the scene and tell you something about who lives there. In fact, the architecture of the house creates the style, but it is the "doorscape," the levels, steps, color, lights, and planting, which complete the picture. Do you want it muddled or clean? And this goes for the whole garden. So the entrance is perhaps an introduction for what is to follow.

"Once out, which way do I go. Is that the front door, or the one I can't see round the corner? The surfacing should tell you where to go and lead you on."

creating a drive

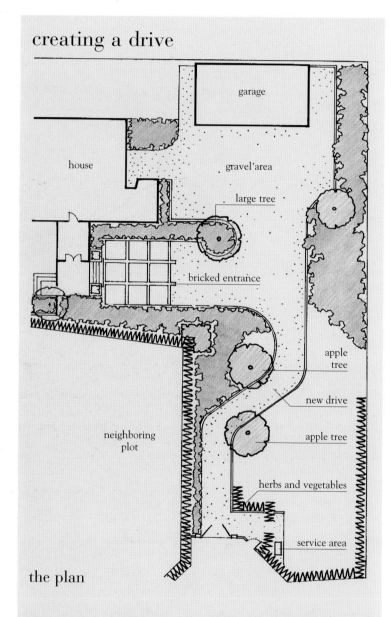

house

garage

gravel area

large tree

bricked entrance

apple tree

new drive

apple tree

neighboring plot

herbs and vegetables

service area

the plan

This plan shows a house with a a double garage. Below the house a piece of the original property was sold off, so a new drive was re-routed between existing trees and divided to provide a decorative front-door entrance with brickwork running through the gravel finish. A service area for the garage and a kitchen entrance to the house were also created. A large tree in the courtyard was linked back to the house with planting, thus dividing the space, and making a feature of a fine horse chestnut tree.

When I get to the front door, it is pleasant to be able to stand protected while waiting for the bell to be answered, and not to have to fight for space with a bay tree placed left and right, or a lethal hanging basket overhead.

By the same token, on departing, the inevitable lengthy goodbyes on the doorstep need a landing by the front door giving ample space for all.

If I'm arriving by car into the driveway of a property, I need to be able to park off the road to open the gate if need be, and I need to stop on going out to make sure that no traffic is coming either way as I pull out onto the road.

I then need to know where to park. In front of the house can be presumptuous, in front of the garage inconvenient. Do I just leave the car floating around in a sea of gravel or is there an obvious pull-in space, with generous room on either side to open the doors of the car to get a plan off the back seat, to let the dogs out, or for a fellow traveler to get in? Leave yourself space to wash the car at the weekend, too.

Once out, which way do I go? Is that the front door, or is it the one I can't see around the corner? The surfacing should tell you where to go and lead you on.

In some houses I visit, there is a fine line between being welcomed and being intimidated by the entrance. Do not overdo the grandeur. I am personally not fond of "in and out" entrances and exits, with a "plonk" in the middle – the dreaded tiered fountain effect. If you want a central island, fine, but leave lots of room to get around it in one clean sweep.

It is important, I believe, that entrances and exits are separated from the rest of the garden. Cars are seldom a visual enhancement, so evergreens will come into play, whether in shrubby form or hedged. Generally, urban gardens have a distinct front and rear. It is only with large properties that driveways can get mixed up with the decorative garden.

Increasingly, the garage is presented to you on arrival – often quite aggressively so, with the house it serves seemingly tacked on. I would suggest that this is to get our priorities confused – particularly when the garage doors are left open revealing what would be better concealed! Where the frontage is narrow it is a difficult problem to overcome. Perhaps the whole frontage has to be given over to hard surfacing and space for vehicles. This need not be too depressing if you start mixing materials and start working with the proportions of the offending garage doors, but you need to interpret it with the overall ground pattern. The hard surface then becomes a three-dimensional sculptural pattern, which you can plant around the edge and use to make a focal point of the front door (see page 178).

The amount of parking space depends upon the size of the household and how many cars it has. If there are youngsters in the family, their friends may have cars, too. If you have a swimming pool, you attract lots of people, and so on. You might also think about space for a boat park, a horse trailer – even an RV?

The town garden invariably has limited parking space, if any at all. Provision is sometimes made by digging out basements – but this becomes architectural rather than garden design.

garage style

TOP Great use can be made of outbuildings on old properties to create garage space or storage, and new garage structures can be erected to create an old effect. This sort of vernacular building looks good when it is located within a country property, and may combine a workshop, log storage, or small stable unit as well. Covered children's play is also provided for.

garden entrance

The entrance gates make up one of the most important elements of a garden. They will be part of the first impression of the garden, so they really do matter.

Entrance gates can be designed just for pedestrians, or may be larger to allow access for vehicles. If they are located near the house, and seen against it, you need to try to work with the architectural style of the building.

"The solution to a welcoming entrance is simplicity, and a sound use of material to provide a firm dry access..."

Increasingly, security becomes more and more of a problem, so the removal of dark shrubbery near an entrance is wise, as is the installation of sensor lights that are set off by someone passing the sensor. It's the shock effect as much as the light that will deter the intruder.

I'm also a great advocate of gravel. It is difficult to walk quietly over this crunchy surface, so it is a great deterrent as well. Where gravel is laid in the passage between houses it will deter a burglar from just "nipping around the back."

The solution to a welcoming entrance is simplicity and a sound use of material to provide a firm, dry access, well lit at night. In hotter climates shade from the sun is a benefit. Your choice of paint color for not only a front door but also for the huge expanse of garage doors is also important. You can emphasize or play down a large structure by your choice of color – bold colors advance, pale recede. Surfacing, too, can affect an entrance enormously. Consider repeating the brick, wood, or stone already present in the structure of the house.

modern carports

TOP A monolithic slab of concrete forms this garage roof and rear wall. It could look harsh and uninteresting, but has been covered very successfully with a climbing hydrangea (*H. petiolaris*).
ABOVE A cantilevered roof provides summer shade for the cars parked beneath it. The surfacing is made of blocks of granite called setts.

creating privacy and extra space for parking and visitors' cars

The original entrance to this forecourt was directly opposite the front door of the house (see plan), and the gravel forecourt covered a smaller area. The owners felt that visitors always parked "on top of the house," and that there was not enough room to maneuver into the garage space. The garden design solution was to extend the driveway by gravelling over an underused area of lawn at the front of the house. A new entrance for this extended driveway was created around the other side of a huge mass of rhododendrons. The old entrance was blocked up, which allowed for adequate parking for visitors cars well away from the front door of the house. This change of access also created more space at the front of the house for the owners to turn and park their cars in the garage.

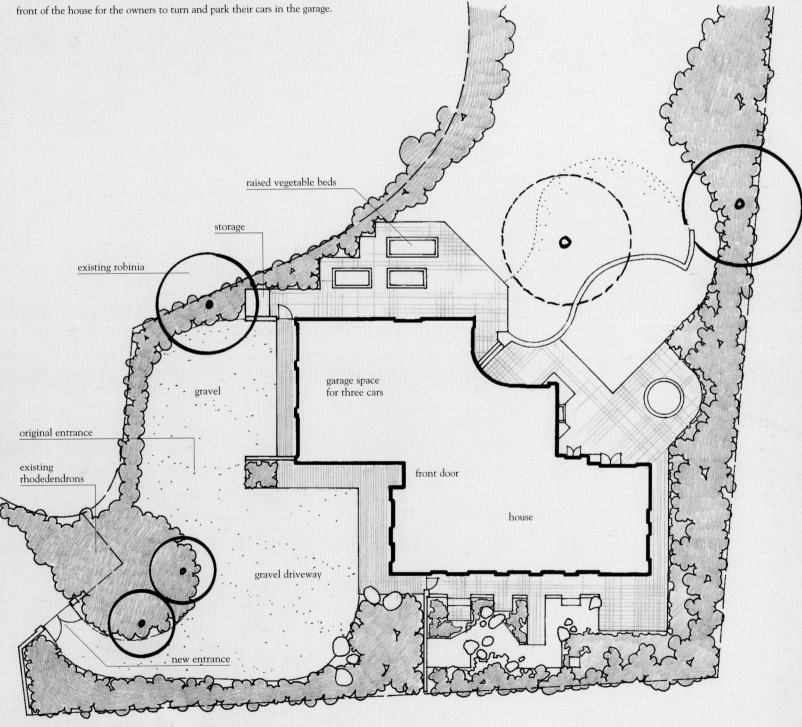

raised vegetable beds

storage

existing robinia

gravel

garage space for three cars

original entrance

existing rhododendrons

front door

house

gravel driveway

new entrance

the plan

surface

Surfaces can be soft – earth, grass, sand, or water – or hard like paving, pebbles, or gravel. It is their texture and serviceability that determine garden use.

Mention surface, and you tend to think of something hard, whether rough and textured or mirror smooth. But surface can be soft as well, consisting of earth, leaf mold, grass, water, or sand. And garden surfaces need not be horizontal either, though as a covering for paths and courtyards we tend to think of it as such. It is the quality and the serviceability of each type of surface that determine how we evolve our garden plan. Their relative cost is a factor, too, and into this equation we must add the labor involved in laying the surface as well.

There are soft surfaces and there are hard ones, with possibly a few in the middle – if gravel is laid loose, for example, it is is a hard material, though it provides a soft surface – the noisy burglar deterrent discussed before.

In most of western Europe we take grassland to be the norm, since it grows so easily in our temperate climate. In fact, it has to be grazed or mown or it will slowly revert to forest, which is our natural vegetation. The forests can be hard- or softwood, depending on altitude, soil, and climate. Above the tree line in Britain heather grows, and where it is too damp for trees we have wetland. Even natural wetland struggles to evolve into grassland and forest, as reeds and rushes, weed and willow attempt to colonize.

We create a hard surface in an area to make what might otherwise be grassland more durable, which with wear would otherwise become wet and muddy as grass gets worn down. We retain patches of grass to mow, creating the lawn.

That soft mown surface is very agreeable, along with the fresh smell that comes after mowing it. Even the stripes left after mowing are all part of the pleasure of this particular surface.

Traditionally, lawn was for the rich man – it had to be regularly scythed or grazed before the invention of the mower in the early nineteenth century. Contrasted with mown lawn, rough grass creates another texture, and much of the joy of differing surfaces is that of textural contrast.

Increasingly, the importance of the lawn within the smaller garden is beginning to be questioned. Lawn maintenance is

soft, grassy surfaces

A mown grass path through a romantic meadow illustrates the different textural qualities of grass used in different ways, here at Christopher Lloyd's garden at Great Dixter in Sussex. There are various techniques for planting long grass with wildflowers (which I will discuss in detail later). Simply by keeping the grass at different lengths – mown and rough mown – you will get some flowers in the rough mown areas at the height to which you mow.

"Increasingly, the importance of the lawn within the smaller garden is beginning to be questioned."

costly in both time and the inevitable chemicals which we pour upon it – to eradicate weed and moss, and to feed it.

My experience of grass is mainly British, and when visitors ask what seed I use, I have to confess I don't know. I buy a mix prepared either for a sunny lawn area, which can take a medium amount of wear and contains no rye grass (the seedheads of which lie down under the mower and pop up again when it has gone over), or I buy a mixture for shade. I could buy a very fine grass, giving me a bowling green finish, which would take little wear, or a hardworking grass-seed mix. Only in exceptional circumstances, like extremely chalky soil or very wet conditions, would I buy a special mix from a seed merchant. If I want wild flowers in my grass mix, I make sure that I get a good proportion of those seeds that grow naturally in the area so as not to disturb the ecological balance.

What does concern me at this stage of a design is maintenance. If you are using different lengths of grass to create a different effect to the mown lawn with stripes, you will need a

rotary rather than a cylinder-type mower. A rotary mower enables you to create a rough-grass look that will contrast beautifully with a path mown through it, and you will get wild flowers in the longer grass to the height you keep the rotary blade. If you constantly chop off the flowerheads as you mow, they cannot make seed and regenerate.

The next important step is to achieve a pattern that a rotary mower can mow, and this will depend to a degree whether it is of the hand-held or sit-on variety – obviously the smaller the machine, the easier it is to manipulate. Right angles are difficult to achieve unless you mow both left and right and then up and down. Flowing lines are easier to manipulate (right).

Examples of other soft surface treatments might include using shredded bark in a woodland area. We are used to seeing bark chips used as a mulch – but they can also be used for soft surface pathways or open areas. Shredded bark is available in a variety of colors from dark brown to bright red, depending upon the trees from which it came. Make sure you pick a color you like.

maintaining a lawn

TOP The traditional striped mown swathe of grass is still very beautiful and forms the centerpiece of many gardens. The maintenance of this type of lawn is high, however, in terms of feeding and mowing. Here we are creating an unnatural monoculture – other plants would grow in it naturally – so "weed" killing requires a further regime. Add irrigation to this in certain parts of the world or at certain times of year, and your lawn may become an expensive luxury.

soft surface solutions

In these sketches I have illustrated how longer grass, whether flowering meadow or not, can be used to create alternative textural qualities. The first (top left) illustrates how rough grass may be used in quite a small garden area, with a mown path around it to give it "trim." Grow bulbs through the grass followed by wildflowers, and then bulbs again in the fall. The size of a suburban garden lawn (top right) is reduced by including a large area of rough grass. Flowing lines provide an easy pattern to mow. The country garden (below) is largely given over to meadow on one side and orchard on the other – though there is still space for children to play.

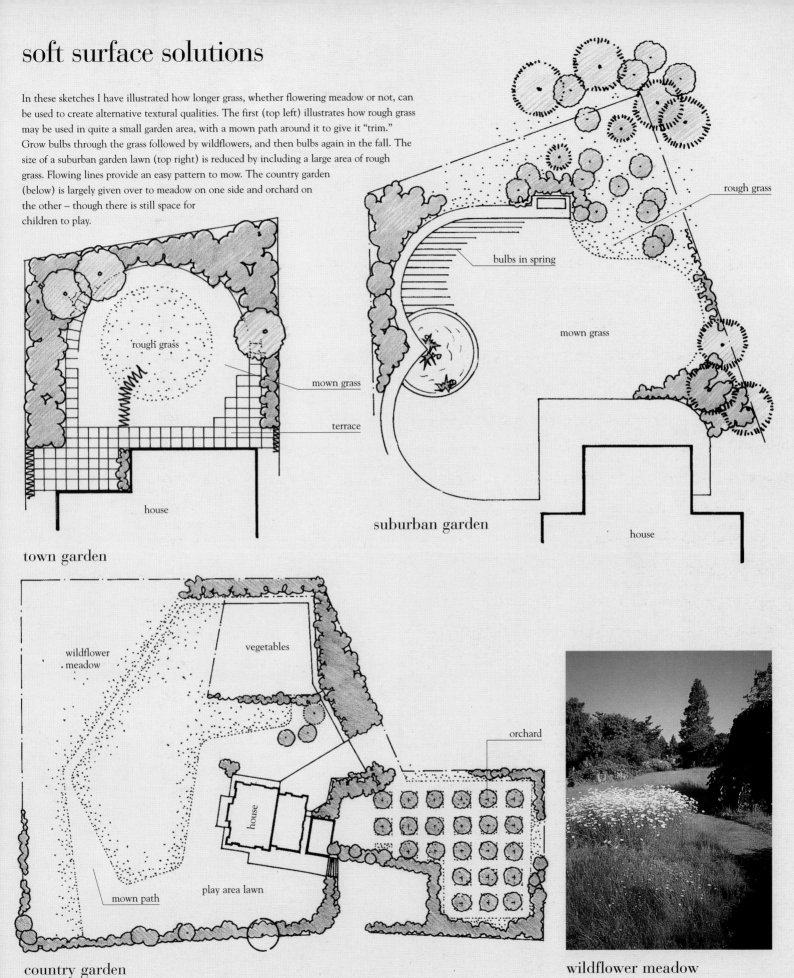

rough grass

bulbs in spring

mown grass

rough grass

suburban garden

house

rough grass

mown grass

terrace

house

town garden

wildflower meadow

vegetables

orchard

house

play area lawn

mown path

country garden

wildflower meadow

grassy ways

An impeccable green lawn looks wonderful, but it needs
to be regularly mowed, fertilized, irrigated, and weeded.
You must be sure you have the time to maintain it.

Today many people are choosing to decrease the area
of high-grade lawn, and to create areas of rougher grass
with paths mown through. The rough grass can be mown
much less often.

You can upgrade from rough grass to flower meadow
on an open site if you wish, but this will need managing.
You will not need to feed the grass, but you will have to
keep to a narrowly timed mowing schedule to avoid
cutting off the flowerheads before they have seeded.

"It is the bits between the planting and what we use as a substitute for grass that present the real surfacing problems."

paving materials

ABOVE In this traditional garden, brick has been laid in a herringbone pattern, within a broad stone edging.
TOP RIGHT A Mediterranean courtyard is paved in a regular stone pattern with a complex pebble infill. This sort of patterning works well to make an imposing building look more human in scale.
RIGHT Bricks or granite setts may be used for pathways, but in this example the paving material runs into broad simple steps of the same material.

In very acid areas it is possible to achieve a rough heather lawn using *Erica carnea*. You will not get any flowers, but a lovely soft, fresh-growth effect, which will take wear. Thyme lawns and chamomile lawns are a bit too decorative to be hard-wearing soft-surface alternatives. They are fine in small areas, though chamomile is hard work to weed. In the decorative garden, we substitute what would grow naturally with hybridized forms or use introduced plants to give a varied green surface.

It is the bits between the planting and what we use as a substitute for grass that present the real surfacing problems.

As a general rule, what is local both looks best and is the cheapest. It looks best because the soil of an area has a direct relationship to the rock below – a local stone or gravel will always have a color relationship with the local soil. An introduced natural material will have a different mineral composition, color, and texture, and will look "foreign." In a highly artificial situation, shock treatment can be fine – but not too often, I would suggest. I wasn't really aware of surface materials when

looking at historical gardens. Italian, French, and eighteenth-century gardens seemed to use hard gravel for their paths. Truthfully, I was not looking at surfaces at all – so horticulturally biased was my background!

It was in the gardens of the architect Sir Edwin Lutyens that I first became aware of textural surfaces and their potential. In a very architectural way Lutyens mixed his materials to create a rich tapestry effect, which when complemented by a Jekyll planting was extremely attractive. Lutyens combined brick, stone, tile, even slate used on edge to form often quite complex geometries. Not until I went to Moorish Spain did I realize their origin. Probably we will never again see this level of skill and craftsmanship in the private garden.

I saw elements of this attention to detail in the surfacings of Dumbarton Oaks, Washington, DC, designed in the 1920s by Beatrix Farrand (who surely knew of Lutyens' work, as she was influenced by Miss Jekyll) and who worked in Britain at Dartington Hall in southern Devon between 1933-1938.

hard ground surfaces

Laying a hard ground surface or path presents a good opportunity for adding textural interest to the garden beyond that provided by plants. Materials such as brick, stone, tile, and gravel can be mixed to produce a rich tapestry effect and quite complex geometries as seen in the Moorish gardens of the Alhambra in southern Spain.

In addition to stone and various kinds of brick and concrete paving, hard surfaces can include wood, such as decking, or railroad ties, which create a chunkier look.

For roof gardens and balconies, you might consider rubber matting to maintain "grip" in the wet. On frost proof sites colored glass or ceramic tiles can create an unusual alternative.

One of the great advantages of mixing materials, which Lutyens did so well, was that huge areas of stone, which in Britain would become slippery in our damp winters, get broken up with smaller elements to provide a better foothold.

It is interesting that many of our roads of the nineteenth century built of blocks of granite called setts had this foot-holding quality. But they were designed for the hooves of horses when pulling drays – to be replaced with smooth asphalt-surfaced roads for faster vehicles as we moved into the twentieth century. Reused in a garden these setts are very handsome. Small square setts are used extensively throughout Europe in beautiful fan patterns to surface many a public open space. True cobbles, which are egg-shaped, tended to be the vernacular surfacing of regions near the sea where they were traditionally taken from the beach. In Britain this is now illegal.

The smaller the element of paving making up a garden surface, the more intimate the atmosphere you create. Interestingly, early Modernist gardens were not concerned with intimacy.

mixed paving patterns

TOP The fan pattern is often used to pave open spaces in European cities. Such a design needs a large space to be visually successful.

LEFT A simple pattern, obviously part of a greater overall one, using granite setts and mosaic. Note the stones are dry-laid around the base of the tree so rainwater can reach down to the roots.

ABOVE When mixing materials, you need plenty of space, and the pattern should be very clear.

paving patterns

There are proper places for formal patterns in paving, and there are places for a more random mixing of materials to create a less formal effect.

Too strong a paving pattern can be too visually demanding in a small garden. I never mix more than two types of material – otherwise the result becomes hectic.

But large areas of the same sort of paving can appear boring, and this is where I would gently break up the overall pattern. You can, for example, bring brick into a stone or concrete area. Tubs and plants will soften a paved area as well.

For designers the Modernist garden was an intermediary between the sleek horizontal concrete lines of the house and the green of the countryside beyond – quite the reverse of the enclosed spaces of the previous era. Pavings were square and precise, of stone or the new material, concrete.

As a student of the 1950s and 1960s, in post-Festival of Britain (1951), I was very enthusiastic about this new exciting material. The older generation, of course, still much influenced by the Arts and Crafts movement, thought of concrete in terms of air-raid shelters, bunkers, and defense cones, and worse still the new architecture, some of which, it has to be said, was pretty grim, all culminating in what became known as New Brutalism.

Flourishing on a thriving postwar building boom, the Cement and Concrete Association was a great patron of the designers Geoffrey Jellicoe and Sylvia Crowe, who designed the gardens at their headquarters at Wexham Springs in Buckinghamshire, where magnificent receptions were held. The Association produced literature on the latest use of concrete

concrete pavers

TOP A modular pattern of concrete squares filled in with granite setts on the angle.
ABOVE More granite setts with precast concrete slabs used both within a pattern and to construct a shallow step. Granite setts were increasingly available as the surfaces of nineteenth-century roads were replaced.
RIGHT A courtyard garden of the late 1960s in which the modular building is re-interpreted in a Mondrian-like pattern of water, gravel, grass, and concrete.

"I now went through my Mondrian phase, using concrete slabs to create a grid pattern, using grass or watery infills, and completing the concept with colored gravels."

around the world. We were really hooked. A publication of 1971 by Dr. Gerard Daumel called *Concrete in the Garden*, proselytized: "Precast concrete has no need for imitation, for it develops its own aesthetic qualities and, along with technical and economic advantages, it offers a considerable range of variety and adaptability." Who needs "old-world" brick and stone, we thought? The market began to be flooded with concrete slabs of every shape, color, and size, which were far cheaper and simpler to lay.

This time, too, saw the emergence of the garden center, which produced a huge new commercial outlet for hard surfaces. I now went through my Mondrian phase, using concrete slabs to create a grid pattern, using grass or watery infills, and completing the concept with colored gravels. In dark London gardens I substituted white gravel for small muddy patches of lawn – it certainly cheered things up! On the old dome site on London's South Bank – under the site of the British Airways London Eye – the architect Theo Crosby built a structure to house an international conference of architects in the 1970s.

edgings

Edging is only necessary where it has to retain something. Used unnecessarily around an area of paving, for instance, it becomes like a fancy pie crust. And indeed many nineteenth-century tile edgings were laid deliberately to create that type of effect.

But gravel needs to be retained when it is used to edge a path or a drive, and brick or concrete edgings set in concrete will do the job. Wooden edging will tend to rot after a time. Metal edging is very crisp and neat but expensive. In rural settings, large logs or old railroad ties can be used.

"In dark London gardens I substituted white gravel for small muddy patches of lawn – it certainly cheered things up!"

For the garden, I used great strips of colored gravels on either side of Crosby's structure with banners flying. I used concrete in my first Chelsea Flower Show garden (sponsored by the Cement and Concrete Association). Everything was about structure and pattern.

These very structured designs needed strongly architectural plants for contrast. The work of Mien Ruys in Holland was highly influential – she combined both a concrete look at the garden scale with a strong use of plant material.

For the first time I began to understand what architectural planting was all about. I had escaped from two-dimensional structure and was now moving forward into three-dimensional design form. But the relationship of plant material to structure and their varying visual strengths is, I think, important. (I will deal with planting styles later). I need to acknowledge the influence that Beth Chatto's Chelsea Flower Show exhibits had on me in the late 1960s and 1970s. There I saw how to put plants together for their shape, not for their flower color. Near Beth's inspirational stand was that of Mrs. Desmond Underwood who

gravel surface areas

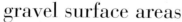

TOP In my own garden I use the local gravel as a basic medium, planting through with self-seeding perennials; combined with architectural features and planting, the mix of hard and soft elements is very pleasing.
ABOVE Different-colored gravels used in concrete aggregate create an exciting stepped contoured effect.
RIGHT Gravel replacing grass in this Dutch garden links the structure of the house with architectural decking surrounding a pool to which it leads.

essentially bred and exhibited pinks – so everything was pink or red or white and gray. They were lovely, but I felt they always looked insipid by comparison, because they lacked structure.

As a reaction to the structural look of the 1960s and 1970s, with perhaps an overemphasis on the use of concrete, there was, during the 1980s, a return to the softer country-house look, which was due to a number of reasons. An improvement in the British economy allowed a greater number of people to consider living in the countryside, or having a second home there. There was also a resurgence of interest in the work of the architect Sir Edwin Lutyens.

Of course, Lutyens built many of his houses in stone. When crushed to provide gravel – as seen so often in mellow Gloucestershire gardens – the two blend together beautifully to create an all-over effect. Add to this the soft qualities of planting that Miss Jekyll advocates and you can instantly soften the effect. This was much more in keeping with the countryside, for which there seemed to be an increasingly romantic leaning.

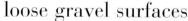

loose gravel surfaces

TOP Gravel used as the ground medium, as it was traditionally, beneath an avenue of pleached lindens.
LEFT This coarse gravel backfills the steps, which have wooden risers. Used in this way, gravel drains itself.
RIGHT Around an octagonal pool the garden designer Caroline Egremont has constructed a Mediterranean-type garden – growing cypress, lavender, iris, and citrus. The effect combines geometry in layout with softness in the selection of plant material and its use.

*"...a local stone or gravel will always have
a color relationship with the local soil."*

loose gravels

There are as many types of gravel or pebbles as there are types of rock around the world. Some are hard and some are soft. Colors vary from white through to black, with all shades in between. Gravel is crushed rock from a quarry. Pea gravel, is river-washed, shore-dredged (illegal in Britain), or dug from pits that were once under water. Gravel has a sharp edge; pea gravel is rounded.

When making a choice, I would advise you always to use what is local. Local materials always harmonize best with your surroundings and your soil.

> *"It is only after traveling and seeing stone used a million different ways that I have begun to appreciate its use not only as walling and gravel, but also as individual rocks, pebbles, or boulders as garden features."*

Currently, there is a revised interest in the use of gravel as a surface material, increasingly at the cost of lawns, which are expensive to maintain and difficult to justify in environmental terms. The modern use of gravel has moved away from the country-house look. Gravel has now become a growing medium for self-seeding native plants. It is at the forefront of new gardening techniques, particularly "steppe"-inspired gardening where plant associations are much freer (see page 272).

Stone is regarded by Modernists as being too rustic, a bit too Arts and Crafts. It is only after traveling and seeing stone used a million different ways that I have begun to appreciate its use not only as walling and gravel, but also as individual rocks, pebbles, or boulders as garden features.

There are broadly two sources of rock, although many different geological types of it. It may be quarried, or you may have it as a natural outcrop (if you are very lucky). It may be water-worn

and rounded, either by a freshwater torrent force that pounds the rock and wears it round, or by the sea, where it occurs as beach or dredged pebbles. Rounded rocks are also found in higher, drier areas where they have been left behind by glacial action as the ice cap receded.

I believe decking, now a popular garden surface, originated from the American boardwalk. In the past I saw it used to create decks onto the garden and to disguise level changes. In Britain at that time, lumber was prohibitively expensive. But over the last few years, quality wood has become cheaper, and the deck has really come into its own. The wood for its structures is now readily available, and a deck is quick and comparatively easy to construct, and creates an instant effect. All are very positive aspects of its use. But to make this surface hardwearing, the detailing needs to be robust and well-constructed, and when it is used in a rural situation (to which I think it is more appropriate than in an urban one), the size of the planks needs to be increased to keep the deck in proportion with its landscape setting.

how to use boulders

in a jagged landscape

in a smooth landscape

These two sketches show how different stone might be used. A decorative placement of sharp rocks (top), quarried from the hills beyond – perhaps with planks and crushed quarried rock from the same source, which would be sharp gravel. In a more gentle landscape (below), rounded water-worn stone is used to create a beach effect of boulders of various sizes, used in association with rounded pebbles of the same sort. Both techniques are viable in a garden, but make sure you are creating the correct "feel" for your location.

using rocks and gabions

TOP A natural rock grouping beneath an olive tree. For the student of landscape, the study of such a natural composition by drawing it (photographing is too quick) is vital.

LEFT A comparatively recent commercial introduction is the gabion, seen here used in a show garden designed by Christopher Bradley-Hole. A gabion is a metal cage in which stones are packed to produce building blocks, cutting down on the labor of craft building such a wall.

"You can now buy squares of assembled decking, not unlike paving, which has a place in the small garden."

There was a time when wood used outside in Britain became very slippery in winter – with moss from dampness rather than frost. But this hazard can now be eliminated by grooving the planks to provide a stable foothold.

You will see from the photographs shown here that decking can be used in various ways according to the run of the planks. It can be edged with wood to give it a trim, or left without. You can now buy squares of decking, not unlike paving, which has a place in the small garden.

I have always associated decking with docks and the lapping water visible between the horizontals. Indeed, used over dry land, what happened underneath the deck was always a problem, since weeds quickly got established. This has been more or less eradicated by the use of black plastic sheeting. Apply a layer of pebbles over the sheeting to hold it in place, carefully disguising the edges, and weeds will no longer be a problem.

It is, of course, vital that the base structure beneath a large area of the decking is securely set in concrete.

ideas for small gardens

TOP A zigzag in robust proportions in the style of the traditional Japanese garden.

ABOVE Decking used to bridge a small pond in an urban garden leading to a dining terrace. The simple planes of wood are nicely contrasted with architectural groupings of plant material.

RIGHT Broad decked stepping terraces leading to a handsome lookout in a Swiss garden by Anthony Paul, who uses wood beautifully in his garden designs.

decking

The wooden deck has come into its own in recent years, and it does create a clean and crisp surface effect. It has also become a bit of a "makeover" cliche, thanks to television garden programs. Unless it is very precise and beautifully detailed, wood generally fits better into the rural or suburban scene. I associate decks with water, too.

Decking can be very useful in gardens where you need to make a smooth transition between levels, and for smaller roof-terrace and balcony areas. Of course, these need to be detailed extremely well, for safety's sake.

wall surfaces

There are as many types of walling around the world as there are mineral rock types. When you add brick, adobe, render, wood, and concrete as alternatives, the choice of wall surfaces becomes almost limitless.

Walls have always provided security and shelter, and most of us would love to garden within a sheltered walled space, but the cost of constructing a wall is often prohibitive. A wall can also help to cut down urban noise (particularly if it is used in association with running water), so a short run of wall can be an excellent investment.

structure

The garden designer can design a successful terrace area by covering it over with a year-round light-filled structure like an arbor or conservatory.

One of the reasons why I loathe most of the current crop of garden makeovers on television is the degree to which they focus on building things – on structure. In reality I find it quite hard to persuade a client to build. A terrace, a few steps, even a pond may be just possible – but a building, either as a folly or for more practical reasons, is almost impossible – even a short run of wall is very hard to get built.

And of course it is all to do with price, not entertainment – that's the crunch. Building is expensive – not necessarily the materials with which you build, rather the labor to get it done.

Perhaps I am being too harsh – and if I come down a notch or two, we do build with wood quite often – the arbor, or a carport structure.

And then again I think that many garden designers are not able to detail a structure. Some of the television constructors have to be builders, and history never relates whether they are conforming to building regulations and/or planning permission. It is not really the garden designer's job to know about

reinforcement or foundations for large structures – although I have found basic architectural knowledge useful.

Where the garden designer does come into his or her own is in that area of structure between inside and outside – the conservatory, the loggia, and the arbor. And although we might not specify the conservatory structure in great detail, we do often try to influence the general look of it, pavings in and out, plantings in and out – creating a feeling of wellbeing in this high-activity area in a garden (or increasingly on a roof).

My feelings on conservatories are somewhat ambivalent. They always seem either too hot or too cold. But there is much more to it than that, and it comes down to deciding the function of the place, and then exploring from that how you might style it. You should stick to one look – too often I see quite inappropriate house plants mixed with plants that require cool temperatures. Many conservatories have little to do with the garden in that they are presented as extensions to the house – carpeted, furnished, and heated as part of the same unit. If this

waterside platform

In a garden overlooking Lake Ontario, Canada – by Darren Schmahl – this structure hangs out over the lake in a spectacular fashion. Such a structure needs proper engineering for total safety. The arrangement of slabs of stone to create steps up to the platform makes a simple transition from the rocky shoreline from which the structure projects.

attaching conservatories

Available in all shapes, sizes, and styles, conservatories can be "tailored" to fit most situations urban or rural, at ground or roof level. Made of glass, they can add warmth to a house through solar energy – but their temperature can drop equally quickly, though this can be alleviated by double or even treble glazing. Shading in summer and adequate ventilation might also be necessary, for if you are growing plants in your conservatory they need a circulation of air as well. Broadly speaking, the larger the area under glass, the easier it is to manage horticulturally and the more useful it is domestically – it all depends upon the degree of use that you anticipate for this additional structure.

Conservatories were traditionally "painted" white – they can now be treated, avoiding constant maintenance, and may be any color. Their structure might be aluminum or wood. Seek a specialist to advise you – research the types of conservatory available, and explore all the possibilities for its use.

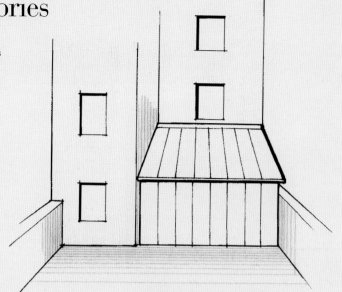

small lean-to conservatory

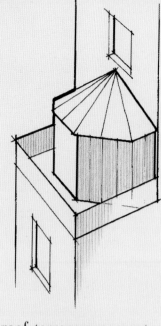

roof-terrace conservatory

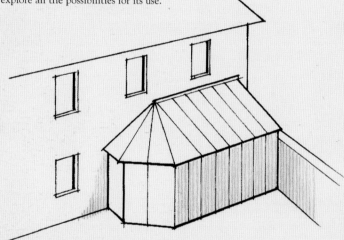

large rear-elevation conservatory

hexagonal conservatory

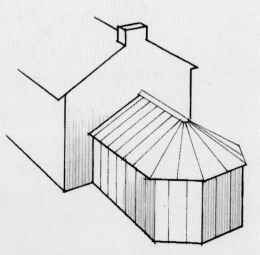

end-wall conservatory

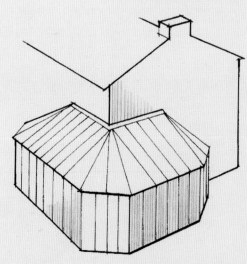

corner conservatory

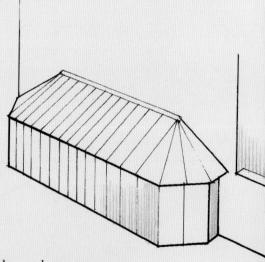

lateral conservatory

"You should always make your conservatory or greenhouse as large as possible. The smaller the structure, the more fluctuations you get in temperature."

is your choice, I would advise you to keep plants to a minimum, since the necessary maintenance (spraying, watering – and subsequent dripping) can be messy.

Other conservatories are treated as summer rooms and winter storage for garden furniture and the like. But this need not preclude their use as a greenhouse with a place for seedlings and potted plants. Indeed, a conservatory might combine these functions with being decorative and displaying flowering plants as well.

The last two uses are really our concern – for their well-being is to do with aeration and irrigation, both of which can be automatic. You should always make your conservatory or greenhouse as large as possible. The smaller the structure, the more fluctuations you get in temperature.

If your aim is to create a decorative effect, choose the upper and lower temperature limit for day and night, and the humidity, and then research plants that can grow within these parameters. Usually the warmer the temperature, the more moisture is needed, and this increases the likelihood of disease.

conservatory extension

A neat urban conservatory extension that is sympathetic with the overall style of the house, and makes a satisfactory transition into the garden. Note how the glazing of the conservatory reflects the proportions of the long windows of the original part of the house. To achieve this, a run of glass has been inserted beneath the house extension's roof line, and this glass sits against the flat-faced brick wall.

greenhouses and conservatories

Conservatories are primarily for sitting in, and greenhouses, as the name suggests, are for growing plants. This does not mean that there cannot be a certain amount of overlap – but people and plants do not necessarily require the same temperature and humidity.

For both plants and people, you need to keep a steady temperature, and the larger the structure the easier this is (though windows and ventilators for air circulation can now be computer-controlled).

The artificial environment means that watering and drainage and a high standard of general maintenance are necessary if you are to grow plants successfully.

"Usually the warmer your temperature, the more moisture is needed, and this increases the likelihood of disease..."

The reason for this is that you are creating an artificial subtropical environment – which needs shade and moisture (and probably double, if not treble, glazing).

The cool conservatory (which in Britain is in its prime in late winter and early spring) becomes quite difficult in summer as it gets too hot unless you have a lot of air flowing through it. It is perhaps better almost emptied, until the first frosts force half-hardy plants to be returned inside. The previous owner of my house set up a cool conservatory in an old tomato-growing

glasshouse – which I continue. The roof opens up and the sides come out to get a breeze through. Still air encourages disease. I plant directly into the gravel ground of the glasshouse and grow plants that are marginally hardy and prone to frost damage. Then I underplant with spring and summer bulbs. These plants require a lot of watering, of course – but also winter pruning, since plants grow very quickly in these sheltered conditions. (To maintain the flow of air for the plants' wellbeing in summer, I top-ventilate and take out some of the glass sides.)

airy interiors

TOP This sort of structure makes a pleasant occasional sitting place. Plant spring bulbs early in pots to create a fragrant foretaste of what is to come in the garden. In summer, geraniums and pelagoniums give color and interest.
RIGHT In my own conservatory, I grow plants for shape, to create an exotic effect in this warm environment. I also plant good clear blues and yellows to set off all the greenery.

summerhouses

A summerhouse can become the focal point of a
garden, but it can serve a wide variety of functions
– as toy storage, a dressing-room, or as somewhere
to house the pool filtration equipment. A quiet
summerhouse with a view of your garden is a great
place to relax and even to work, but it must be big
enough to be practical.

*"A good conservatory needs quite a
lot of knowledgeable management.
Don't overreach yourself."*

Then there is the period conservatory – Victorian or Edwardian – each quite different in character.

Many town dwellers now decide to cover over their small gardens with a structure since traffic noise can spoil an urban garden. Lack of sunlight might be another factor – in which case, you grow plants for shade, such as ferns. Again, temperature and moisture availability will be a determining factor. A good conservatory needs quite a lot of knowledgeable management. Don't overreach yourself.

When it comes to a greenhouse, it is much better to site it away from the house so it is free-standing and receives maximum light and air. Structures can be built of cedar and painted, or from aluminum, and should have a pitched-roof. Another possibility is the lean-to, which is usually designed for fruit cultivation.

A greenhouse can have glass to the ground if you want to grow in the ground – or it can be half brick with glass on top if you are growing plants on shelves. You may also need a cold

conservatory design

LEFT A very stylish urban conservatory room used as a summer dining room leading to an equally chic outside sitting space on a decked area. The very simply shaped forms of structure and furniture are echoed in the clipped forms of box grown in pots. There are Japanese maples on either side of this conservatory, designed by Luciano Giubbelei.
ABOVE This conservatory addition fits neatly and in proportion to the rear of this country house.

frame, invaluable in the British climate at least, for hardening off plants prior to planting out in spring.

Other possible built structures include the loggia. In Britain we think of it as a period addition to the house – and useful, too, for taking off boots and cleaning dogs' paws.

But in sunnier climates the loggia provides shade, and sometimes shelter from rain to create an outside living room through the summer months. It can have sofas, a carpet, lamps – be a true room outside in fact. Sometimes these loggias need screening against mosquitoes and other bugs – it depends on where you live. A loggia just has a roof – no sides.

I never could understand what those little bandstands were in lots of American gardens. They are, I gather, a sanctuary (when screened) from very aggressive bugs at certain times of the year as well as a garden feature.

The arbor is a garden structure more commonly seen around the world, and it comes in many forms. The earliest were relatively light structures, used as grapevine arbors.

outdoor structures

TOP A freestanding garden structure covered in climbing roses provides shade in summer and becomes an attractive garden feature.
ABOVE An open loggia at the side of a brimming pool becomes a focal point in the garden for summer parties, and protects guests from the cold dew that descends in the late evening in Britain.
RIGHT In sunnier climates the loggia provides daytime shade and even a siesta location.

"But in sunnier climates the loggia provides shade, and sometimes shelter from rain to create an outside living room through the summer months."

loggias

The loggia – popular in the Edwardian era – is a structure that modern building designs rarely include. It is the space created below when you build an overhanging upper story and support it on columns. If the loggia is deep enough (and the summer hot enough), it can be furnished, becoming a genuine outside room. If you add overhead heaters, lighting, even an open fire, the space can be used for many months of the year.

small structure solutions

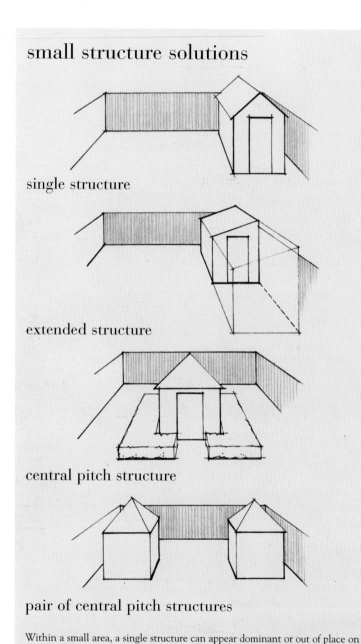

single structure

extended structure

central pitch structure

pair of central pitch structures

Within a small area, a single structure can appear dominant or out of place on the site. However, if you extend the structure with the addition of an arbor or a greenhouse, the new building becomes more purposeful. A single building with a central pitch structure, becomes more appealing still. With two central pitch structures you could create a small formal garden in between the buildings, or add walls around the perimeter of the site and a central gate between the structures leading to a service area beyond.

The detailing and style of an arch or arbor can come in many forms. Arbors can be massive, using old house beams to create an ancient effect – or they can be light and airy – almost invisible – with the plant material more important. But plant material can be heavy, and a sound structure is vital. The visual balance between the structure and weight of the vertical with the weight, width, and height of a horizontal is something of a conundrum. I don't think that there is any particular equation; much depends upon whether your arbor structure is free-standing or connected to another building, and the weight of plant material that you wish to grow upon it.

A more common problem, in British gardens at least, is the positioning of garden buildings, for which we seem to have a mania. Garden buildings can be for storage – for bicycles, for the mower, all manner of household goods. They can be log piles, a tool shed, or just a retreat from the rest of the family. The structure can be purely utilitarian, like a shed, or decorative like a summerhouse; and then there is the small greenhouse, which

"Bring your small structures into your basic design. Too often, they are last-minute additions imposed into a scheme."

might be either utilitarian or decorative. Where should they be positioned in the garden? Do they need access?

Curiously, the smaller the building, the more difficult it often is to site, since the scale of its height outweighs its dimensions. Established, preferably evergreen, shrubs give scale to the garden and can be used visually to support or even hide these odd structures, many of which, due to their function, need to be near the house but are at odds to it in terms of their scale and the materials from which they are built.

In a small garden, I think that an arbor or arch can be used sometimes to bind these structures together – and then with painting or staining they can blend them into the background.

Bring your small structures into your basic design. Too often, they are last-minute additions imposed into a scheme. Lucky the country-house owner who has outbuildings – not only are they useful – but they can be extremely attractive as well. They help somehow to mellow the house into its site, and the space between is often attractive, providing a sheltered microclimate.

pleasure pavilions

TOP LEFT A gazebo in this Sussex garden restoration provides not only an office upstairs, but a sheltered pavilion below, while also being a terminating feature to a water canal in the garden, with a view to the grounds outside it.

ABOVE Children's play equipment can provide a really garish intrusive structure in a garden – but this small Tudor playhouse, surrounded by a flower garden, is an attractive solution.

utilitarian structures

Log piles, carports, workshops, tool sheds, compost bins, and the like can all too easily clutter a garden. At one time these sorts of outbuildings were built deliberately in the same style and at the same time as the main house, and they fitted into the overall picture; now we rely on a well-placed shrub and a bit of trellis to conceal them. The secret is to plan the position of utilitarian structures early, to group them together, and to organize paths and paved areas around the structures to service them.

planting

In the twentieth century there were many changes in the ways gardeners chose to use plant material – some of which were the result of environmental concerns.

I was a latecomer to the decorative use of plants, although I trained in commercial horticulture (it would be called amenity horticulture now). My landscape training was concerned with history and with design, and covered only an extremely limited range of "useful plants."

In retrospect, this was the effect of Modernism, and the Modernist selection of plant material primarily for overall shape to act as a foil to the strong architectural lines of public buildings or community housing. In the 1970s, a designed private garden was seen as something of an indulgence for the rich. Hence *House and Garden* magazine's concern, in that period, for grandeur – with a famous name dropped in for good measure if possible. There were no other regular publications like this – only "hands-on" gardening reference manuals.

This concern for shape, I think, was further fostered by a postwar Scandinavian influence not only in furniture and architecture, but in woody interiors, too, with a massive use of house plants. I remember pages of ravishing line and tint drawings of plants by Gordon Cullen in the *Architectural Review* – a technique I desperately tried to copy, but with outdoor plant material. I was working for Brenda Colvin on fairly traditional garden layouts at the time – it was all a bit frustrating since there was no scope for applying my new technique.

Brenda Colvin has, I fear, been rather passed by. She was an established prewar landscape architect and a founder member of the Institute of Landscape Architects, who started up again in the postwar period. Her practice bridged the gap between the dwindling tradition of grand private gardens and the modern profession of landscape architecture. She wrote the first book on the modern landscape's wider implications, as early as 1947, entitled *Land and Landscape*, followed by another standard, *Trees for Town and Country*. Brenda was a great plantswoman, rather in the Jekyll tradition. She was also skilled in planting design – rendering some of her drawings in the early 1960s taught me a lot.

Another Scandinavian concern was the use of hedging for wind shelter and for patterning in the garden, which was to be

textural planting

Our concern for the use of plants has moved away from an interest purely in flower color. In the limited area of a smaller garden, form, shape, and texture have to come into play, and we now think about winter color and seedheads, too. The current approach to planting is a reinterpretation of natural groupings – but without an exclusive use of native plant material. In some fields, land management has taken over from horticultural technique.

"Brenda was a great plantswoman, rather in the Jekyll tradition. She was also skilled in planting design – rendering some of her drawings in the early 1960s taught me a lot."

seen when looked down upon from the house. I'm particularly thinking of Sorensen's Kalundborg Cathedral Square, a design that has always stuck in my mind.

You can see another beautiful example of Scandinavian work, that of Arne Jakobsen (no relation to Preben Jacobsen) at St. Catherine's College in Oxford. There he makes use of a counterpoint between hedges and walls, which is both formal and challenging.

Currently this effect can be seen in some of Preben Jacobsen's very sensitive plantings – for example, those at Farnborough College of Technology in Britain.

The prime current exponents of this form of green gardening are the two Belgians, Jacques Wirtz and his son Peter – whom I have already mentioned. Together they are creating a clipped hedge formality – which is not new to northern France and Belgium – mixed with a soft underplanting of material. The finished result seems to fuse the best of both the Formalist and Romantic traditions in a new and exciting way.

awareness of landscape

The work of the landscape architect Brenda Colvin, in whose office I worked during my apprenticeship, was a great influence. On the left are some of her planted beds in her garden in Gloucestershire. She managed to bridge the gap between diminishing grand garden-design patronage and a growing need for an awareness of landscape and the garden in its setting. These issues she outlined in her book *Land and Landscape* published in 1947.

architectural planting

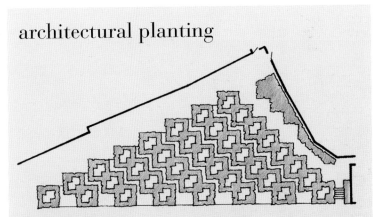

hedging creating abstract patterns

formal paving and box hedging

The realization that plants could create an abstract pattern became clear to me seeing Carl Sorensen's (1899-1979) design in hedging for Kalundborg Cathedral Square in Denmark (top). Arne Jakobsen's (a fellow Dane) landscape work at St. Catherine's College in Oxford (1960-1964) is remarkable for its simple formal approach (above). This approach, with box-edged beds, still has great appeal, and it is often used in town gardens – the shapes remain to provide structure throughout the year. And, indeed, many period houses call for a straightforward surround. Tall yew hedges provide excellent wind shelter, and it is from them that the formal approach takes shape.

green gardens

At the other end of the spectrum to the plantsmen are the green gardeners. Their specialty is to create spaces using plants. This "green patterning" may often be designed more to be seen than to be explored.

This concept has been transposed from the Renaissance gardens of Italy and northern France, though much scaled down. Later green patterns have become more abstract, and with age and the correct clipping maintenance, they bring some of the extraordinary shapes of Surrealist fantasy into the garden.

"The prime current exponents of this form of green gardening are two Belgians, Jacques Wirtz and his son Peter..."

There had always been a simmering interest in planting design in the garden world fostered by postwar writers like Margery Fish, Vita Sackville-West, Lanning Roper, Peter Coates, and Rosemary Verey. But this was nothing like the 1980s Jekyll explosion, which seemed to mirror middle-class lifestyles of the period. Growers such as Beth Chatto and garden lecturers such as Christopher Lloyd began to tour and enthuse the world with English gardens and gardening techniques. I went on one such tour with them to Australia. Gardening also started to take the United States by storm.

And this brought another twist. The American interest in perennials, perhaps first appreciated in the English border beds, turned into the realization that many of those plants were American natives from the midwestern prairie.

The working partnership of Jim van Sweden (the designer) and Wolfgang Oehme (the plantsman), practicing out of Washington, DC, started to plant gardens throughout the U.S. with perennials, similar to those seen on the prairie.

classical influence

ABOVE This very structured layout by Jacques Wirtz is quite extraordinary. It breaks all the rules of symmetry one expects in a classic layout with plant material controlled this way, while still managing to exhibit huge classical influence. Regular clipping and maintenance are required to maintain the crisp shapes.
TOP RIGHT The mellow roof and the many chimneys of an English country house form a backdrop to the rich, mainly perennial plantings of a Jekyll style of garden.

country cottage

The original workers of the land grew fruit, vegetables, and herbs in their cottage gardens. And of course some of those same plants flowered. Only since the nineteenth century has a higher standard of living allowed larger numbers of purely decorative flowers to creep into the mixture as well – and indeed to overtake the earlier function.

This gentle profusion of often small-headed flowers throughout the season became the aspiration of most everyday gardeners and influenced country-house planting, too, right down to the present.

the prairie experience

I was aware of the cold of the upper Midwest in winter, but it is only recently that I have experienced summer there, too, when it was incredibly hot and humid. Frustrated by the performance of introduced species, gardeners from Chicago to Minneapolis are beginning to work with prairie plants that will withstand this heat and drought. Another revelation was the variety of species within the prairie landscape. In late summer I walked through a heady mix of tall flowering perennials, and all manner of grasses. It is this experience which the landscape architects Oehme and van Sweden have picked up on. In the garden they designed (below), they have mixed a host of perennials that grow wild on the prairie.

The partnership aimed to create what they aptly named "Bold Romantic Gardens" – a name they also gave to their earlier 1990s publication on garden design. I think their role in creating the prairie look was a worthy follow-up to the writings of Rachel Carson in the early 1960s in stimulating environmental interest in the U.S. – though somewhere sandwiched between the two there had been "xeriscaping" from California, which was at the time heralded as the technique for planting in areas of water scarcity.

"The American interest in perennials, perhaps first appreciated in the English border bed, turned into the realization that many of those plants were American natives from the Midwest prairie."

It is interesting that both Jim van Sweden and Wolfgang Oehme have a European connection. Jim van Sweden, with Dutch parentage, but growing up on the edge of the prairie, trained in Holland as a town planner. Wolfgang Oehme was from East Germany and was a disciple of the late great plant- and nurseryman Karl Foerster. Karl Foerster can probably be described as the father of the modern interest in a freer use of plant material. It was he who reintroduced many perennial ferns and grasses to enrich the designer's palette of usable plant material – and so influenced van Sweden and Oehme.

Another earlier American influence on planting design was the landscape architect Jens Jensen (1860-1951), who pioneered the use of indigenous plant material in the Midwest. Karl Foerster, a contemporary of Jensen, also influenced a generation of German landscape designers and plantsmen by his writing on landscape architecture.

prairie-type planting

This style of planting is obviously for the larger-scale garden. Though similar to the meadow style, it includes a wider range of plants, which thrive in a damper situation than would be suitable for steppe-type planting. Prairie plants tend to be more vigorous than meadow ones and may include perennials and grasses growing as high as 6-10 ft (2-3 m) each season.

Prairie planting management is quite complex and may require occasional burning to stimulate the natural cycle of regeneration from dormant seed.

"Rosemary Weisse...would impoverish soil that had previously been improved to allow for the development of wild perennials and grasses."

native species

ABOVE A natural woodland edge planting in Britain of foxgloves (*Digitalis purpurea*) mixed with lady ferns (*Athyrium filix-femina*).

RIGHT A view of Rosemary Weisse's "prairie" planting in Munich's West Park. To establish this European prairie look – which is very different from native North American prairie – plants are grown in a soil medium that has not been enriched or amended in any way.

Although Foerster did not exclusively use indigenous plants, he was interested in the way in which plants grew naturally.

Foerster was a great influence on Rosemary Weisse as well, who, working in Munich's West Park from the late 1980s, began to turn previous decorative horticultural wisdom on its head, since her technique was at odds with the convention of constant soil enrichment. Rosemary Weisse made the point that native plants – in which there had been an increasing interest – need a poor, unimproved soil. She would impoverish soil that had previously been improved to allow for the development of wild perennials and grasses. These were not grouped but rather drifted, allowing the self-seeded look to develop – a technique that is now known as "matrix" planting. At West Park Rosemary Weisse created a host of different plant associations in differing soils – wet or dry – which she calls prairie or steppe planting.

And so slowly we developed not only a feel for plants associated with a particular soil, but an increasing awareness of wider environmental issues as well.

meadow planting

There is a spontaneity to natural meadow planting that
is inspiring more and more garden designers. There are
many meadow types, but they tend to be on poor soil that
has not been fertilized other than by manure from grazing
animals. Grazing can be an important part of meadow
management – whether by domesticated or wild animals.

The creation of a meadow takes time, and you must
have the necessary space. You need to observe attentively
the natural development of the meadow, and apply
specific land management techniques that work with it.

*"Many designers...have become obsessed with flower
color, often to the exclusion of all other plant attributes
– like shape, form, leaf texture, fruit, and seasonal effect."*

Working from this environmental concern is another school of plantsmen I call "the colorists." In Holland one might include Ton ter Linden and Henk Garretsen. In Britain the mood is fostered not only by a latter-day Jekyllian theory of color, but also by the planting and publications of Penelope Hobhouse, Nori and Sandra Pope – and by a growing school of garden photographers as well. The current star of the plant firmament is a Dutchman, Piet Oudolf, who is combining all these influences to transform the look of the garden.

I have to confess that I find the look slightly alien in Britain. We are a country of seasons and need to celebrate this in our planting. I am happier with British versions of the Dutch idea as realized by another writer on the subject, Noel Kingsbury.

Our British climate is quite mild and benign when compared to the more extreme climate changes on the continent, and that means we can grow a huge range of both native and introduced woody plants that, in my opinion, we should not be without for the sake of color interest.

"the colorists"

LEFT Two leading garden writers in Britain, Nori and Sandra Pope (they are the authors of *Colour by Design*), have a wonderful commercial garden at Hadspen House in Somerset in which they have an enormous mixed – though mainly perennial – border bed of graded color, within a walled garden.

ABOVE The perennial garden created by Ton Ter Linden, a Dutch painter by training, offers glorious but subtle color shifts within the beds.

"the colorists"

Starting from the work and writing of Gertrude Jekyll, who was influenced by the cottage garden, many designers, writers, painters, and photographers have become obsessed with flower color, often to the exclusion of all other plant attributes – like shape, form, leaf texture, fruit, and seasonal effect.

The mainly summer mosaics of plant material they create, write about, paint, and photograph are often superb, and it is to that standard that many ordinary gardeners seek to aspire – all too often forgetting the limitations of their particular site.

*"The current star of the plant firmament is a Dutchman, Piet Oudolf,
who is combining all these influences to transform the look of the garden."*

Furthermore, in Britain we expect June to be the high spot of our gardening season – occasionally it is, as roses come into bloom. July I always think is better, when the perennials come into flower. But with an increasing European influence in plant choice and a growing use of grasses, the high point comes in August, continuing until the end of the year – which is even more reason to combine the British way with a European one.

My own particular slant on all this is the use of gravel as a planting medium – or rather more as a mulch. It is the technique I will describe as that of the steppe. The gravel is consolidated and you plant into it. Self-seeding plants, liking drought, pop up where they will, and I remove the others – so it's a constantly changing look, admirable for herbs as well. Also, this steppe planting technique provides a useful alternative to grassy areas that need constant maintenance.

These newer techniques may look wild, but they still need managing, and instead of the old routine of digging over and enriching the soil before planting, we have the reverse.

inspirational plantings

ABOVE This project by the plantswoman Beth Chatto is in her own garden in Essex on the site of a former parking lot. Planted in dry gravel, she has incorpor-ated a Mediterranean flavor into steppe and gravel planting.
RIGHT At Green Farm Plants in Hampshire, Piet Oudolf has planted in great drifts, using grasses, distinct flowerhead shapes, and color. This technique is outlined in his book *Designing with Plants* – which offers an inspirational approach to plant combinations.

garden and setting

Although often overlooked, the newer prairie and steppe planting techniques ought to relate the garden to its natural setting, since the right technique for the particular location will create a far more complementary, ecological association between the plants and the landscape. This garden design at Lady Farm, south of Bristol, was created by its owner Judy Pearce with Mary Payne, and does just that. Broad swathes of shrubs and perennials fit into the scale of their landscape (right). The wetter hillside areas (top right) are treated to prairie-style planting. while the drier areas are designed as steppe (bottom right).

planted shrubs and perennials blend with the landscape

woodland walk

bottom lake

top lake

cove

▷ N

farm building

formal garden

courtyard

wild flowers

stone bridge

old steppe

bridge

new steppe

fountain pool

conservatory

entrance drive

position of tennis court before regrading

old prairie

waterfall

stream

hosta walk

new prairie

the plan

prairie-style planting on the hillsides

steppe-style planting in drier gravel areas

"So where to start if you are new to this game of planting?
First of all you do need to know about plants, but you also need
to know about your soil, so you can select your plants."

If you want a maintenance-free garden (it is a contradiction in terms, incidentally), concrete or pave it.

So where do you start if you are new to this game of planting? First of all, you do need to know about plants, but you also need to know about your soil, so you can select your plants. I believe that a good starting point, other than asking neighbors or the garden center, is to compile a local vegetation notebook, and begin to identify what is growing in the area, on the fallow field, in the park, or by the river. With the leaf and flower identification you will learn the plant's soil requirements, whether it likes wet or dry conditions, whether it is deciduous or evergreen, its flowering time, and so on. And it is this technique that you apply to choosing plants for your own garden. You are no longer striving for exoticism, rather for a perpetuation of the spirit of the place in which you live.

I would suggest you should not contemplate any soil removal or replacement prior to planting. Clear the ground of invasive weed very thoroughly – if it is a virgin site, this might

gravel planting
In my own garden in Sussex (above and top right), I often plant into a gravel medium. Biennials self-seed and are protected in the gravel throughout the winter. In time, the plants spread to create an entirely new picture, which I control fairly strictly to achieve this sculptural and colorful look. The foreground plants shown above include *Eryngium giganteum* 'Miss Willmott's Ghost' and *Verbascum bombyciferum*, a particularly fine gray strain of our native mullein.

take a whole year, but you will save yourself much work later if you really start from scratch with clear ground. If your clear ground is very dry and the soil very dusty, and/or smelling of cats, you will need to condition it. Work in lots of organic matter, which has the effect of binding together loose dry grains of a coarse or sandy soil, but breaks up a sticky clay or chalk one. In summer, organic matter will help to retain moisture as well.

Traditional wisdom always dictated that you feed your ground, and this is still important when growing fruit and vegetables. But current thinking suggests that you do not feed a decorative garden, because you are changing the characteristics of your soil. Learn from what grows naturally in your area – select plants from your local palette.

The next stage is to obtain a local nurseryman's catalog and start to check what is listed with what you can see at the garden center. Make notes about light, water, and soil needs, but also about growth rates and how high and wide the plant becomes in, say, five or ten years.

planting plan at Denmans

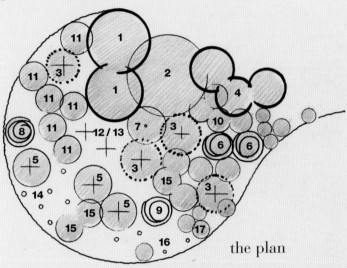

the plan

This wild style of planting contains predominantly gold foliage, mixed in with yellow and white flowers. Lime-green heads of euphorbia and lady's mantle self-seed through it all, as does evening primrose (*Oenothera* 'Fireworks'). Such a planting is a halfway stage between native planting and the romantic bed that gives pleasure through the year with colored stems and grass forms.

KEY TO THE PLAN

SHRUBS
1. *Viburnum rhytidophyllum*
2. *Sorbaria aitchisonni*
3. *Rubus cockburnianus* 'Golden Veil'
4. *Cornus stolonifera* 'Flaviramea'
5. *Rubus thibetanus*
6. *Rosa* 'Blanc double de Coubert'
7. *Rosa rubrifolia*
8. *Rosa rugosa* 'Alba'
9. *Rosa* 'Max Graf'
10. *Hypericum moserianum* 'Tricolor'

PERENNIALS
11. *Inula magnifica*
12. *Crambe cordifolia*
13. *Arundo donax* 'Variegata'
14. *Achillea* 'Coronation Gold'
15. *Euphorbia polychroma*
16. *Aquilegia* hybrids
17. *Hemerocallis* species mixed

INFILLERS
Oenothera 'Fireworks'
Verbascum bombyciferum
White cosmos
Alchemilla mollis
Solidago 'Lemore'
Lily-flowered tulips (lemon)
Fritillaria lutea
Eremurus bungei

steppe and gravel planting

Simulated dry steppe, using gravel as a dressing in which to plant (the gravel provides a well-drained anchor), is a new medium in which you can create a matrix of different plants. Woody plants and grasses can be mixed with perennials and bulbs to create a semi-wild effect that does not need regular cultivation or watering. It is an exciting modern development in garden design, drawing on our concern for the preservation of natural resources and the sustainability of our natural landscapes.

"Learn from what grows naturally in your area – select plants from your local palette."

A beautiful plant dictionary is all very well when learning about plants – but they tend to focus on flowers. I would use a commercial catalog combined with hands-on experience. The dictionary is fine later on when you get into plants, but do not overreach yourself to begin with.

I think that both the student garden designer and the new gardener should start to categorize plants, and then learn them in groups. The categories will start off with your local native trees and shrubs – evergreen and/or deciduous. This provides a background. Now select medium trees, if you have the space, or smaller ones – for foliage, flower and/or berries, their fruit – perhaps just six or so. Then do the same for tall evergreen shrubs, and then flowering ones, selecting medium size and smaller.

Select six subjects that have a strong architectural shape, making a list as you go along. My list would be adapted for chalky gravel (alkaline soil) in the south of England – roughly the equivalent zone of Seattle, though the native species there would, of course, be very different.

This list becomes your basic reference point. Notice that I have not yet listed the flowery subjects – the perennials, biennials, annuals, or bulbs – since they become the icing on the cake and are selected later. The first selection of plants is to do with the relationship between the areas of the garden plan. You then proceed to build up the masses three-dimensionally. Actually this is where the fourth dimension of time comes in – because of course your plants will grow.

This is one of the few art/design forms where this moving fourth dimension of time affects your forward thinking. If the plants are too far apart in your planting plan, they will not block out the wind and provide shelter – but if they are too close, they smother each other too quickly and need to be thinned. Decide therefore on a time span – I would suggest that five years is ample for a knitted-together look for the smaller garden. For a larger one ten years, though if you are planting slow-growing hardwood trees like oaks or cedars in your park, you will need to think much further ahead!

site-specific planting

TOP When choosing material for a bed, flowering perennials are not the only option. Here, a selection of local grasses have been chosen for a hot dry site in a front garden. They create a soft natural sweep along the edge of the path to the front door.
RIGHT The plants of the Arizona desert have strong architectural forms, which contrast with the simple house. The plant shapes are an adaptation to the great summer heat and lack of moisture in this region.

planting for location

In nature, planting occurs spontaneously – seeds or spores being carried by wind, water, or wildlife to land by chance in a variety of locations. The seeds only prosper if they are suited to that location or habitat. Nearly every climatic zone around the world has its own vegetation mix, adapted to hot or cold conditions, wet or dry, and to the local soil type, whether acid or alkaline. Early agriculturalists destroyed much of that natural vegetation cover to graze their livestock or grow crops. Settlers introduced species they were familiar with – often to the detriment of the native flora and fauna.

Slowly we are rediscovering what the natural balance of our native vegetation might have been – and we are beginning to transpose this knowledge into a new horticultural language and aesthetic.

"Start with the trees – ultimately it is their scale that relates your garden plan to the scale of your house."

planting among trees

ABOVE Existing trees are often present, and they need to be taken into consideration when landscaping the site with plant masses or areas of water. Choose strong leaf forms that are suitable for shady areas below trees and are not overpowered in the landscape.

FAR RIGHT Lower branches can be removed from trees in wooded areas to allow light through so that plants grow beneath. Underplant with large drifts of material to match the scale and proportions of the trees.

I should say here what I personally think the function of a garden might be. I do not think that it is a plant museum. My objective is not to grow one of as many different types of plant as possible to prove the success of my horticultural technique; it is rather to create a restful backdrop to look into or be in, and to be animated in my absence by lots of birds I can see from indoors. Huge varieties of plants, with clashing forms and foliage, with masses of vibrant color, are not what I am about. I seek a quieter way that respects the land on which the garden sits, both physically in my husbandry of it, and visually in my design and subsequent plant selection.

I now categorize my plants according to their function. I think this is always necessary, no matter how you style your planted infill. Start with the trees – ultimately it is their scale that relates your garden plan to the scale of your house. The trees might even be there on the plot already, in which case your plan has to adapt to them anyway – or you may have someone else's trees or neighboring woodland as your backdrop.

In this case, your selection might only be for a smaller flowering tree that you would position in front of them.

Where you are starting from scratch, remember to think in terms of a tree's span as well as its height – since what you plant beneath the tree starts in sun but ends in shade.

Try not to create an unrestful effect with too many different types of trees. Clashing gold and purple foliage give interest perhaps in a show garden initially – but in maturity are somewhat indigestible to be with all the time. Within a wider setting variegated and colored foliage can look very artificial. If you are not in a softwood area (usually identified by acid soil), planted conifers can look artificial and instantly say "humans about" as well. So keep cross-referencing back to your native trees as a guide. You will probably realize that in most parts of the world the native plant selections are not huge, and one particular tree mix is usually dominant. Only in the largest of landscape gardens would this affect you directly – it is just an interesting point.

designs with existing trees and shrubs

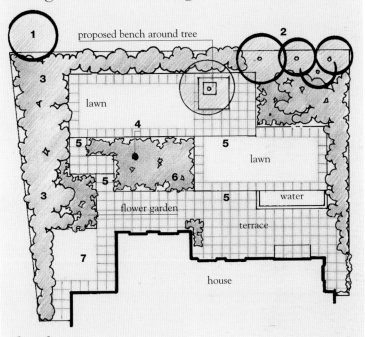

the plan

The garden plan evolves with existing trees and vegetation as part of the new proposed design scheme. In this case the existing trees include a row of old conifers, an apple tree, and a neighboring yew (*Taxus baccata*). I have planned a wooden bench seat around the apple tree to make the tree into a prominent feature. In front of the house, I have created a wide stepped entrance and a long, low pebble pool. Planting screens the fence surround for extra privacy from neighboring gardens. Areas of lawn allow play space for children. Both the change in levels and the planting scheme have evolved together to produce an intergrated design.

KEY TO THE PLAN

SHRUBS
1 Existing yew tree in neighboring garden
2 Existing conifers
3 Screen shrubs
4 Ornamental jar
5 Step up
6 Flower garden
7 Service area

"Try not to create an unrestful effect with too many different types of trees. Clashing gold and purple foliages give interest perhaps in a show garden initially – but in maturity are somewhat indigestible to be with all the time."

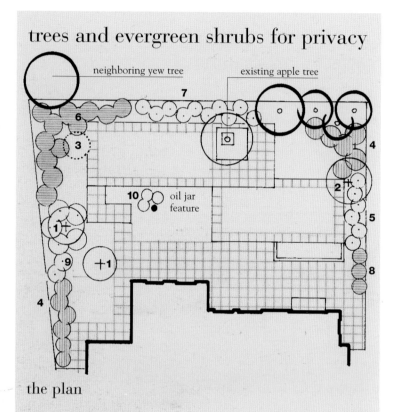

trees and evergreen shrubs for privacy

neighboring yew tree

existing apple tree

oil jar feature

the plan

Here again is the same garden (see page 285). The existing special tree is the apple tree with the wooden bench seat surround. I have suggested two gray-leafed *Sorbus aria* 'Lutescens' to block the view of the neighboring houses on the left and a winter-flowering cherry (*Prunus autumnalis*). The cherry would show up well against the conifers. Other specials might include fastigiated Irish yew (*Taxus baccata* 'Fastigiata') to read against the neighbor's yew on the south side, with three *Phormium tenax* behind the oil jar feature in the flower garden. The skeleton planting is of evergreen shrubs, which would provide year-round interest as well as privacy.

KEY TO PLAN

TREES	EVERGREEN SHRUBS
1 *Sorbus aria* 'Lutescens'	**4** *Viburnum tinus*
2 *Prunus autumnalis*	**5** *Escallonia iveyi*
3 *Taxus baccata* 'Fastigiata'	**6** *Elaegnus x ebbingei*
	7 *Pyracanthus* 'Mohave'
	8 *Pyrancanthus* 'Teton'
	9 *Pittosporum tobira*
	10 *Phormiun tenax*

The skeleton shrubs I select next help define the garden's plan. If I am creating a formal layout, I will choose hedge material – but more probably I will not be so rigid – I am usually selecting large, simple masses of plants to enclose my garden, to block a bad view, hide an ugly building, or screen the garden from a prevailing wind. These shrubs, in the main, will do their job best if they are evergreen as well. Yew, box, holly, and viburnum are my locals, to which I can add cotoneaster, pyracantha, and various pittosporums, but there are a lot of species to choose from in each genus.

I have found that this system can be applied to most projects, although plants will change. It's the sheltering concept that is so important, particularly on a large site exposed to wind or the sea – until you have a screen belt, little will grow inside.

When planning garden schemes in North America, I have had to learn about conifers, since broadleaved evergreens that survive winter are limited. But the shapes work there – it is their home, whereas in southern Britain they are difficult to place.

It is at this stage, before getting to your selection of decorative plants, woody and herbaceous (woody remains through winter, herbaceous dies down), that you decide the style in which you are going to plant your plan. At this point, I would also explain the planting outline to the potential client and have pictures ready of the trees and shrubs that I intend to use.

The decorative groupings are made up of shrubs such as lilac, philadelphus, and hydrangea which will show up against the skeletal background. I am still interested in the shape of these subjects – the vertical, the horizontal, or the rounded – for even if they are all deciduous, I still see their outline through winter. But, I am now starting to think about flower color as well – and times of year in which flowering occurs.

Part of your garden styling exercise will have been to think through what palette of plant color you want to use. The house attached to the garden I am using as an example of a successful planting plan (see artworks pages 286–292) has a lot of blue in its interior color scheme, so I am making a feature of this color

tree color

TOP The snake-bark maple *Acer Pensylvanicum* has obvious stem attraction, but in the fall its leaves turn a wonderful copper shade contrasting with a lead-colored garden figure by Marion Smith.
ABOVE The golden-foliaged *Robinia pseudoacacia* 'Frisia' can be overused – I like it so much I do it myself. But in this New Zealand garden a pair of trees are used to create a lovely setting for this seating arrangement placed beneath them.

in the garden, too, mixing it with lemon, yellow, white, and a touch of purple.

I like to plant my shrubby material in drifts of color – one mass with another – in as romantic a way as possible. If you are starting out on planting design, however, and have a limited knowledge of plant material, use larger masses, and concentrate on leaf shape and texture (contrasting shape against shape) rather than getting too involved at this early stage with flower color. Use twiggy yellow broom with soft gray mounds of senecio, for instance, and then in the next area contrast spiky iris with round-leaved bergenia. Let these big masses of material complete your collage of designed garden shapes.

This architectural style can read very strongly and work well in town, where there is a lot of masonry. Remember that foliage plants do flower as well! When you have the confidence, you can start to combine the architectural with the romantic look if you wish. After all, that's what the inclusion of topiary does in the old period-house gardens. This romantic style, when

working with shrubs

TOP This is a good mix of plant shapes, evergreen and evergolds, through which later perennial masses grow. They include *Elaeagnus ebbingei* 'Limelight,' *Lonicera nitida* 'Baggesens Gold,' yucca, *Phormium tenax*, with a small broom in the foreground.

ABOVE This woodland planting of decorative material is mainly of azaleas, whose brilliant colors light up the spring garden in cool temperate conditions.

"Start off using only six main species spread about, to hold the concept together, contrasting the flowerhead shapes of perennials and grasses."

selected carefully, can be attractive throughout the year as long as you include evergreen plant material in the scheme.

In both these styles, you plant in groups – fluid in the romantic, quite rigid in the architectural.

To create more of a mosaic of plant material, consider the matrix type of wilder planting that copies nature's way and seems to grow at random. What holds such a concept together is the repetition of species used, but it also needs quite careful planning out on graph paper. Start off using just six main species spread about, to hold the concept together, contrasting the flowerhead shapes of perennials and grasses. With this technique you do not cut down plant material and put it "to bed" in the fall, but allow the plants and seedheads to remain until early spring for the birds to feed upon and therefore contribute to the ecology of the garden. Only as bulbs appear do you clear the flowerbeds. Your selection of plants will depend upon your location. Consider what perennials and grasses grow locally, then plan your matrix using that knowledge.

adding decorative infill

the plan

In the same garden (see planting plans on pages 285-286), the decorative infill is constituted by small-scale woody plants rather than perennials, which would be too large for the scale of the garden. I have drifted the decorative shrubs in front of the skeletal material, so you would get a different plant combination when the grouping is seen from different angles. Any holes in the planting in winter, which might reveal too much fence or wall, I cover with vines. Think orientation first, some vines prefer full shade, such as climbing hydrangea, or half-shade, such as honeysuckle, or full sun like climbing roses. Some like clematis prefer to have their roots in the shade and head in the sun.

KEY TO THE PLAN

DECORATIVE WOODY SHRUBS

1 *Buddleia davidii* (white)
2 *Philadelphus coronarius*
3 *Hydrangea* 'Annabelle'
4 *Phlomis fruticosa*
5 *Viburnum davidii*
6 *Rosamarinus officinalis* 'Upright'
7 *Rosa* 'Little White Pet'
8 *Rosa mutabilis*
9 *Senecio* 'Sunshine'
10 *Hedera* species
11 Climbing rose (client's choice)

plantsmanship

For years the content of one's garden and the way in which the plants were grown was of more importance than the overall effect. Indeed, to establish and encourage your collection you hedged off the garden to shelter it, denying the countryside in which it sat.

You enriched the earth to encourage your plants, but lost the plot along the way – and you completed your exotic adventure with an Italianate or Japanese garden layout. This style of gardening and plantsmanship is perfectly acceptable and has contributed in a major way to an extraordinary horticultural boom. It just is not my way any more – I have moved on.

> *"Used in a random way, annuals and bulbs can fill up bare soil between a matrix planting of young perennials and can also extend the season of interest."*

matrix planting with perennials

the plan

In the same garden (see previous plans), I have enlarged the flower garden area and suggested a mixed "matrix" type planting of repetition. This starts with *Helleborus corsicus* early in the year and progresses to *Geranium sylvaticum*, with *Anthemis tinctoria*, *Gaura lindheimeri*, and asters for the fall. Foliage color is provided by gray helichrysum (curry plant) and purple salvia. Textural lightness is provided by the grass *Deschampsia caespitosa*. Through the planting bulbs you can grow tulips and *Camassia*, and alliums with hyacinths (*Galtonia candicans*). In late summer, I would plant white foxgloves around the shrubby plantings, and lady's mantle in the light shade.

KEY TO THE PLAN

1 *Anthemis tinctoria* 'E.C. Buxton'
2 *Aster divaricatus*
3 *Helichrysum italicum*
4 *Gaura lindheimeri*
5 *Geranium sylvaticum* 'Mayflower'
6 *Helleborus corsicus*
7 *Salvia officinalis* 'Purpurascens'
8 *Deschampsia caespitosa*

I mentioned earlier the designation "prairie" for areas with moist soil and "steppe" for dry soil areas, but this is very broad. In reality there are different types of both. The dry steppe look, for instance, verges upon the Mediterranean, although the latter will have more bulbs in it, the former more grasses. We saw earlier how popular grasses have become among garden designers, although I think that the public has some way to go before appreciating their subtleties.

Some of the most spectacular effects can be created almost instantly in a new garden by sowing annuals and infilling the beds with bulbs. Used in a random way, annuals and bulbs can fill up bare soil between a "matrix" planting of young perennials and can also extend the season of interest. An extra plus is that bulbs, in the main, will repeat and annuals will self-seed so you do not have to repeat this process. Within a couple of years, the decorative shrubs and evergreen material will have started to mature and fill out the flowerbeds so the need for fillers in the gaps between young shrubs is diminished.

perennial planting

This is a fine example of the newer mixed way of planting perennials with grasses at Tuinen, Netherlands, by Piet Oudolf, in which both texture and color are considered along with a contrast in flower shape – the cone-shaped flowerhead, the flathead, the spire. Since Oudolf's plantings are left through winter in his beds, these shapes can be read through frost and even under light snow cover.

10

water

In a garden plan, water may be used in a formal way in association with a terrace or building, or it may simply nestle into the landscape.

I don't think that I can have a very watery birth sign, for water doesn't excite me the way it obviously does many people. And yet when I think of gardens I have built, water does usually come into them – for it provides a powerful draw to the eye and should ideally be the base level from which everything else works. Water, I keep pointing out to clients, should be at the bottom of a hill – not halfway up it. I think you can fake it – with earth shaping and planting – but have a care. It can look very strange if you get it wrong.

I think I first started playing around with fresh water as a child; I would construct dams in local streams and provide steppingstones across the result. I eventually built a rectangular pond at home in concrete and became interested in pond life, pond weed, and marginal planting.

Another frequent watery experience was rowing at school on the River Wear, surrounding Durham cathedral and castle. This was truly magnificent landscape set off by water and the sound of running water, as the "eight" in which we rowed took off.

I think that it was during my National Service spent largely on Salisbury Plain that I first discovered chalk streams on weekend hikes; I loved their clarity and the sway of fronds of water crowfoot in the current, like long tresses of hair. Early in my work, the making of small ponds in London gardens was the usual use for water. Clients always have an obsession with the dangers of water and children – quite rightly – and I raised the pond surrounds to make them safer.

Only when I started to design country gardens, often the weekend home of an initial urban contact, did I start to think about creating larger, natural water shapes. By this time I had started to fly, and the many forms of water from the air have always fascinated me. I'm the person with the blind up when you want to watch the in-flight movie! Agricultural pattern and land forms intrigue me as well. From the air, I could see the oxbow lake shape I had learned about at school. I really began to appreciate organic curves in the landscape, and the shape that water currents can carve out of the ground.

natural pond
This is a butyl rubber-lined natural pond – the result of the pond construction work (see page 303). Much of the planting is native and grows very well in this site, so it needs clearing out every five or six years, when plants are divided and reduced in size. This is about ready, as the central water lily mass has become "clumped." Nevertheless, such a pond becomes a great sanctuary for wildlife in the garden, with bats and swallows swooping down to drink.

The Santa Barbara landscape designer Isobelle Greene derived her inspiration for the pathways through a conservatory she was redesigning at Longwood from the braided waterway through a gravel water course – and this was something of an enlightenment to me. Since then, I have always asked students to sketch natural shapes – even if it is only tracing the bark patterning on trees! The sweep and curve of organic shaping relates directly to land form. It has been generously carved out of the landscape and molded by wind and water – and there are few stingy little wiggles within it.

This is my starting point for thinking about the use of water naturally within a landscape. For many years I was lucky enough to have the great water expert Anthony Archer-Wills living nearby. He was an inspiration – and a great practical help to me. I could simply draw up a plan of a stretch of water and hand it over to Anthony to build. By this time, the availability of butyl rubber (used as a pond liner) made the creation of a whole host of water features easier – but the mechanics of using it I left to him.

natural water forms

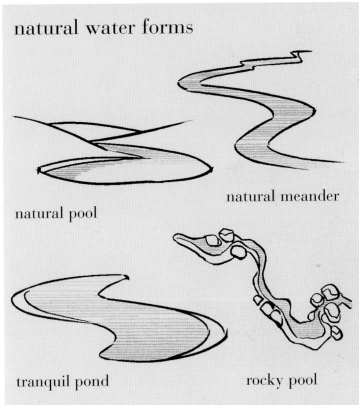

natural pool

natural meander

tranquil pond

rocky pool

When creating a pond or a lake, give it the feel of your particular region. It could be a gentle curving shape (top left), or taken from the formation of a meandering stream in the landscape. You can create a pond with rounded boulders and a pebble beach, or use more dramatic rocky shapes (bottom right). And to this you will add the appropriate planting mass for different water depths and perimeter treatments. Use marginal damp-loving plants for the area at the pond edge (see page 303).

carving the landscape

TOP I have always been intrigued by the shapes that water carves for itself within a landscape. Here, a winding river in Britain is about to join up in the middle and abandon a piece of itself, which will become an oxbow lake and eventually dry out.
LEFT Mudflats in a tidal estuary create ever-changing patterns from which the garden designer can learn how to use shape in the landscape, though on a much reduced scale, of course.

natural water

Many "natural" garden pools are not convincing.
Only where water is running do you naturally get
beaches of rocks, pebbles, or sand. If the water is
still, there will always be growth pressing in from
the perimeter, with reeds and rushes for wildlife
in its shallows. So getting the shape of the pond
right has a lot to do with creating an illusion of
running water.

"Naturally water collects as it runs off from surrounding hills – it may or may not be fed by a stream. You are copying this principle on a reduced scale."

There is much more to creating a natural-looking piece of water than meets the eye. First of all, the outline has to work with the landscape pattern – the fields, hedges, and woods – so the water looks natural in its setting. Water naturally collects as it runs off from surrounding hills – it may or may not be fed by a stream. You are copying this principle on a reduced scale. The pond you make will look best at the lowest point of your property. If you are creating a stretch of water of any size, have a surveyor take levels so you know where the waterline will come to all around the pond. This might seem obvious, but it is amazing how deceptively your ground level changes – you won't necessarily get the shape you were expecting. The finished result will look very natural, however, and will sit very comfortably in its landscape setting.

You may have to consult with local municipal planners when proposing an expanse of water of any size in the garden. When work starts, they may fear you are making a sand or gravel pit, and as they are responsible for the local environment and the

relaxing by water
ABOVE If a pond is correctly sited and its edges are convincingly natural, the chances are you will probably want to sit by it. I think this decked platform is pleasantly understated and in keeping with its location. The deck area is surrounded by cleft hazel fencing for safety.

water and levels

Water should find its own level, which is naturally at the lowest point of a site. But what looks as though it is level often is not – so take levels accurately before starting to dig the hole for a pond. Then think about what you will do with the topsoil and the subsoil (they should not be mixed). When the site has been dug out and the soil excavated, it always looks like a huge amount of material to deal with as the soil is no longer compacted.

   In constructing this pond in my own garden, I learned by experience. The cross-section shows the profile I was trying to achieve. Stage 1 – digging the pond and lining it with soft sand, which was cheaper than a commercial cushioning material. Stage 2 – lining the pool with butyl rubber to make it watertight. Stage 3 – creating an excavated shelf beneath the rubber liner – this enabled the construction of a low retaining wall on the garden side of the pond, which creates a crisp pond edge. Stage 4 – the bankside of the pond is planted with marginal, damp-loving plants before moving up the bank to a more usual planting of garden shrubs. The marginal plants create a transitional area from wet to dry land.

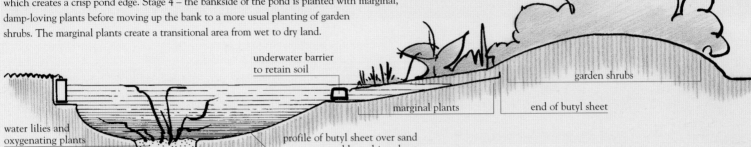

underwater barrier
to retain soil

garden shrubs

marginal plants

end of butyl sheet

water lilies and
oxygenating plants

profile of butyl sheet over sand
or permeable cushion sheet

cross-section through pond

stage 1

stage 2

stage 3

stage 4

look of an area, they may need to be sure that you share their views and are not creating an eyesore.

Then you have to consider what to do with the material you have excavated. If you are not removing it completely from the site (which can be expensive), it needs to be incorporated into the existing landscape. Removing topsoil, working in subsoil, and then bringing back the topsoil can be a tricky operation when the site is small.

If you are laying a butyl sheet over a large area, I would advise you to get professional help, or at least have your project checked. When constructing a local lake, we found that water started to accumulate in the clay beneath our butyl sheet, and it was necessary to install a pump to keep it dry. This can get technical – so check on what you're about to undertake. You may also need a cushion layer between the rubber and the stony soil beneath.

In some areas where there is clay subsoil you can sometimes get away with no butyl sheet. However, stones can work up through the clay lining and cause leakage – and you must also

make sure the pond is kept topped up at a constant level, because where water recedes, the clay will crack as it dries out, and when it fills up again after rain, the pond will leak around the edges. Again, an automatic top-up on a ballcock is easily arranged – but leave it to a professional.

Areas of water do not necessarily need a freshwater feed into them. Water can be perfectly fresh and clear without an inlet, provided you establish a proper balance of plant and water life within the pool. Do not introduce fish or waterfowl too soon. Let your water clear first. Floating bales of barley straw seem to do the trick miraculously – the decaying straw releases water-clearing enzymes. It does not look very nice – but it will clear your pond in a month or two. Do not overplant your pool. Water plants grow quickly, and some can become invasive.

Subconsciously, I think I learned a lot from my field rambles when I was young because I also took on board how water plants grow, and the characteristics of transitional area from wet to dry. In some parts of Britain, natural grass seems to give way directly

small stretches of water

ABOVE Small areas of water are far more difficult to maintain than larger ones. This is a fenland agricultural landscape, drained by a manmade ditch, but its scale is spectacular – we can learn from this.
RIGHT Morning mist clearing from an ornamental lake. The foreground deck would make a peaceful place for contemplation.

"Water can be perfectly fresh and clear without an inlet, provided you establish a proper balance of plant and water life within the pool."

"...the sound of water is often more important than the look of it."

to water – on either side of the slow-moving chalk streams of the south, for example. Where water flows more rapidly, it can create a beach effect of rounded stones and pebbles of different sizes, and where the stone is really soft, it creates sandy or pebbly beaches as well. Notice that the current cutting into a bank creates a sharp edge with the beach on the other side. You can mix plants with a beach effect – although naturally it would be muddy. Nature is constantly trying to grow into a pool of water, with reeds and rushes as the vanguard, and then (in temperate climates) follow up with shrubby willow and alder, which with time become large and form small trees. In the still water itself, the weed gets thicker and the waterlilies closer together – so there is a constant pressure of growth pushing into a pond. The gardener or landscaper has to watch this in the ongoing maintenance of a watery area. Otherwise, you suddenly wake up one morning to find that there is no open water left, the stretch of water has become overgrown with plants, and that your pond is only half the size of the one you started out with.

A last thought on wild water. Where you are creating a stretch of it, make it as large as you can afford. It is an expensive feature, but you will not regret it.

Water used informally becomes part of the overall look of a landscape. But used formally, water can dominate it. This is perhaps a bit sweeping, for I do not remember water as the dominant feature of Renaissance gardens, because the surrounding evergreen oaks or cypress act as a balancing foil – in those gardens, the sound of water is often more important than the look of it. Typical in Renaissance gardens is the sight of water falling, or being thrown up into the sunlit sky against an evergreen backdrop. Sun really brings water alive.

I have an early memory of water reflected from a pond onto my bedroom ceiling, in a house in which I was staying, making quivering Hockneylike patterns that were endlessly beguiling.

I have had a continuing interest in the Islamic garden, my first experience of which was in southern Spain. Water is the key feature of this style of formal garden. The scale varies

the sound of water

TOP With sunlight water can be a great joy – with movement from a waterfall or fountain. It can be fun, too, as illustrated by this arrangement of jets designed by Katherine Gustafson.
RIGHT Particularly attractive in a hot climate, the sound of water is both cooling and refreshing.

formal water shapes

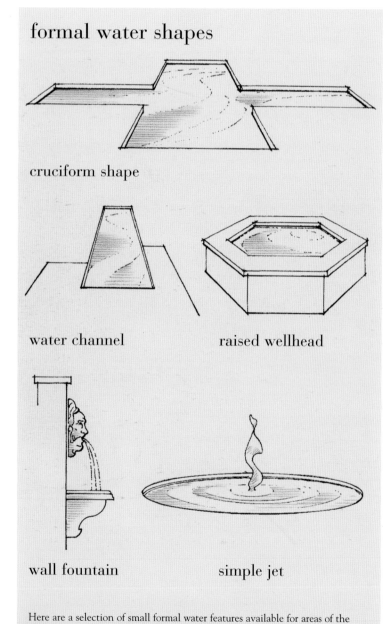

cruciform shape

water channel

raised wellhead

wall fountain

simple jet

Here are a selection of small formal water features available for areas of the garden, such as the terrace where you may like to have running water to create a relaxing environment. The smaller the area of water, the more I think it should have an elevated site – or it may just appear as an insignificant hole in the ground. The wellhead (without the winding gear) and the decorative wall fountain are probably the smallest features that can hold water in an outdoor setting and are suitable for a small town-garden or courtyard area.

according to location, but the importance of water remains constant. Within the traditional village, there is a sequence of priorities for water's use, starting with the head man's garden, then the villager's drinking water, for washing and so on, before finally irrigating the fields and orchards. Within the formal garden enclosure, under the shade of fruit trees, are pavilions for household or pleasurable use, all made possible by the introduction of water. In the Mideast water, is at a premium, and without it there is no life.

Water therefore becomes the central theme of rich man's paradise on earth and takes on the religious significance I described earlier. But the garden was, and still is, used as a retreat from the heat and dust of an arid landscape. Later Islamic gardens used water in a more descending fashion, with waterfalls often dividing up parts of the gardens into individual rooms and functions, though this needed the presence of adequate running water. These quantities of water were available in Mughal Indian gardens in Kashmir, in the foothills of the mountains.

Islamic water shapes

TOP A canal with small central fountains at the Bagh-e-Fin, Iran. You can sense the play of sun and shadow, feel the warm air, and hear the gentle trickle of water.
RIGHT The Islamic cruciform concept, signifying the four rivers of life, is reinterpreted in a British garden. Fountain jets play out from the corners of the central square of pond. The terrace surround forms a square herringbone pattern of brickwork.

"Islamic gardens used water in a more descending fashion, with waterfalls often dividing up parts of the gardens into individual rooms and functions..."

small pools

Small areas of water fit very nicely into a terrace, close to the house. The water can be at ground level, or raised up to make it safe for children.

An edge that is broad enough to sit on (and from which to feed fish) is an added attraction. A fall or a fountain introduces movement, and creates a calming sound, which can be used to help block out traffic noise.

"The amount of water used in those formal layouts depends on the garden's location. Near the mountainous areas of Iran or Kashmir, water gushes and flows..."

The amount of water used in those formal layouts depends on the garden's location. Near the mountainous areas of Iran or Kashmir, water gushes and flows, but in the desert of Rajasthan often the dry cruciform shape of the container, with no water, has to suffice.

My first experience of this wonderful Islamic garden world was the magic of the Alhambra and Generalife in Granada, Spain. Here the scale of garden and enclosure is quite domestic. The effect, with the scent of citrus pervading all, is very moving.

Later, living in Iran, where I had a garden design school, I experienced the Persian version of the water garden. I recently returned there on a garden tour and rediscovered the magic of these places, often so much more significant than the western garden, since they managed in a dry climate to create the earthly paradise of water in their gardens.

Persian water canals actually brim (not unlike some of our chicest swimming pools) with water flowing over the edge of the lip of the pool to be caught in a trap at the base.

channels of water

LEFT A canal of water with a central waterfall feature. The nozzles for the water are a feature taken off the seventeenth-century house which the canal adjoins. The lower pond works independently of the top one, which helps to regulate the flow of water.

ABOVE A static reflecting pool in the manner of the Mexican architect Luis Barragan, whose brimming horse troughs and minimal style have attained iconic status among designers.

"We in the West, albeit on a smaller scale, can learn from the use of water in Middle Eastern gardens."

There is no planting in this water (it is intended to flow and sparkle instead), so it lacks the bucolic effect of a formal British pool of water lilies.

Fountains in these early formal pools worked on pressure. Running or stored water was taken in a large bore pipe, whose diameter was gradually reduced to force the water upward on its release. Huge water displays happened only very occasionally, I suspect. A similar system created this effect in later Italian and French Renaissance gardens.

We in the West, albeit on a smaller scale, can learn from the use of water in Middle Eastern gardens. The design of the container can either be strongly directional across the site (dividing it firmly in two), or on a smaller scale a formal pool can "create" a garden. In a very small dark space, it can act as a mirror and bring light into the area.

In a British garden, I constructed an Islamic-type pool and rill laterally across the terrace (right). A relation of the client had once lived in Iran, which inspired the use of this Islamic-style water feature. Now, any stretches of formal water I create I relate to the examples I saw in Spain and Iran, but in British gardens the scale required is much smaller. I still believe, as I do when planning natural pools, that once you have decided to use water, it is important to have plenty. Apart from anything else, larger expanses of water require less maintenance – the greater volume makes it easier to establish a balanced ecosystem beneath the surface of fish, snails, and plants. Also, large areas of water reflect more sky on their surface and catch more light.

running water

TOP I'm not sure what this watery detail is all about. But there is something I like about this trough overflowing into a lower pool. It creates a moody atmosphere in which light and shade, color and form mingle to great effect.

water garden design

This water garden designed for the terrace of a Lutyens' type house in Britain was inspired by Islamic examples, and those that I have seen in Moorish Spain. Here, two formal square pools are connected across the brick and gravel terrace by a narrow water channel or rill. Water appears in a gentle bubble on the top terrace beneath an existing weeping willow tree – and outside the kitchen door, where meals are eaten in the summer. This pool then overflows, and the rill ripples down to a larger, deeper reflecting pool between the dining room and the sitting room. To maintain the balance in the design, I have introduced a small, formal herb garden at the far end of the terrace beyond the sitting room. Wide steps lead down from the terraced area in front of the house and take you to a pavilion (not shown), which has magnificent views across the surrounding countryside.

main pool

small pool on the house terrace

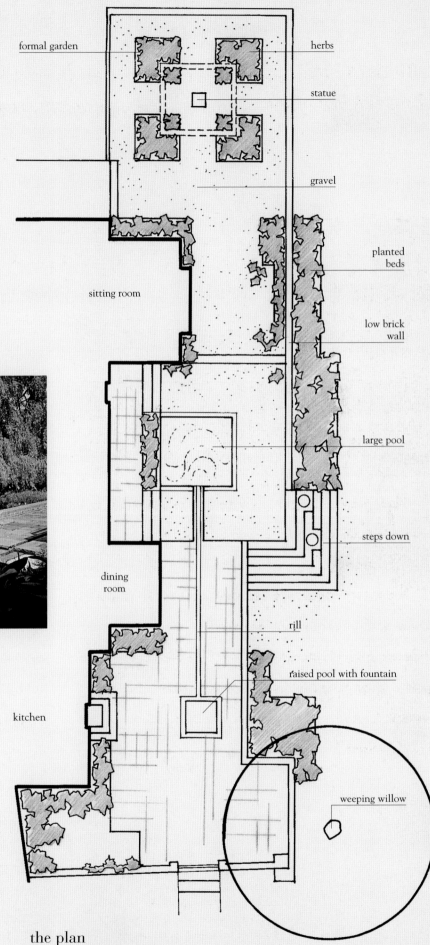

formal garden

herbs

statue

gravel

planted beds

sitting room

low brick wall

large pool

steps down

dining room

rill

raised pool with fountain

kitchen

weeping willow

the plan

water channels

The earliest decorative gardens were created in the
Mideast and were irrigated by water which ran to them
in channels. This arrangement became part of
the Islamic garden tradition, according to which the
channels become stylized into a basic cruciform shape,
and the gardens they watered became known as
"quartered" gardens. The length and breadth of the
channels varied in different parts of the Islamic world.

In the early twentieth century, this tradition was
reinterpreted in some of the garden designs of Sir Edwin
Lutyens – at Hestercombe, for instance – and later in
the century by Geoffrey Jellicoe at Shute House. Today
the water channel is still popular in garden design.

"Running water can block out noise in an urban situation, and it can be located against a wall."

You can raise the sides of the pool a little 20 in – (50 cm) to stop children from falling in – though this alters the statement you are making. Your sheet of formal water can be a canal or even a rill, where the stream is very narrow (in which case it is really only a link between two other watery points), a pond, or a wall-mounted fountain. Canals of water work well in flat landscapes, because they echo the drainage ditch – the natural shape in an agricultural landscape (see page 308).

Water in a small garden has to be used carefully, I think, or it becomes too "dinky" at ground level. Raise a small area, a little like a wellhead, and you almost have a sculptural feature. Running water can block out noise in an urban situation, and it can be located against a wall. It shouldn't be too noisy, however, because the peace of a garden is all important.

I think it important, too, that water only serves one purpose in a garden. It is all too easy to have waterfalls and fountains, colorful tiled surrounds, and too many plants in a frantic effort to "amuse." Simplicity, I believe, is all.

urban water features

TOP In a small urban garden, a raised pool becomes the focal point on a terrace. The sound of a trickle of water blocks out intrusive neighboring noises.
ABOVE A raised pool forms the foundation to the room looking onto it. The doors of the room fold open to provide a lovely summer outlook.
RIGHT Slick architectural use of water, beautifully detailed, with a magnificent colored wall contrasting with a bed of lavender.

swimming pools

A swimming pool is a big sheet of water, often with a large accompanying terrace area. It sits most comfortably in a big, expansive landscape design. For pools in smaller areas, make sure you use masses of plant material to balance the proportions of the swimming pool and terrace. The simpler the pool area, the better.

Obviously, the warmer and more exotic the climate, the more appropriate a swimming pool will be – but for a family with children, a swimming pool provides an enormous attraction, even in a temperate climate. A pool area also has its dangers for the very young, and security needs to be considered at the initial design stage.

Lap or plunge pool, abstract or formal, covered or open? These are some of the questions the prospective owners need to ask themselves – after the price of installing the pool, that is!

style

Style is almost indefinable, but in garden design terms it has to do with selecting the right thing for the right place. It is also a matter of personal taste!

Every year at the Chelsea Flower Show, there are stands galore suggesting all manner of goodies to "personalize your place." Of course it is tempting to buy these things (many of which are very expensive) to scatter about your garden, often in an attempt to rectify a more basic design deficiency – another seat, arch, or urn, even a piece of sculpture or statuary. Remember that a badly cut garment is not rectified by adding too much decoration to it!

Consider one or two basic objects as part of your design. Directional gardens will need a focal point at the end, for instance. Gardens that meander need one or two features of interest to be discovered as you wander, but they need to counterbalance each other within the layout.

It is typically on the terrace that one starts to amass too many garden bits. This can be catered for if you group them, like objects on a decorator's table. But generally the objects need to be bigger, for they are seen against the scale of the garden looking out, and against the scale of the house looking back. Little bits just scattered here and there clutter the place. Think about it as you would for interior decoration, only outside.

At this point I should discuss the merits of using traditional statuary or modern sculpture in a garden. Again, personal preference and suitability come into play. I think many people are deterred from using modern sculpture, not by price, but by having to commit themselves to making a decision on what they like. A piece of classical statuary does not commit you; it is safe. A piece of abstract sculpture is still considered brave. Somewhere in between (it is often very evident at the Chelsea Flower Show), there is a whole range of objects, usually bird or animal, which must be popular. Sentiment colors the picture here, too, which is where sculptures of cupids and cherub, kittens and puppies come in!

In my own garden I have concrete and stone pieces, and fiberglass, too. Anything valuable in lead, even stone, is sadly in danger of being stolen unless it is extremely well secured. I had a stone urn, which I thought well anchored, near my own front gate.

sculptured metal

Many of the exhibits at the annual garden exhibition at Chaumont in France are stylish, and many have a conservation message as well. Sometimes, gardens are developed by students and can, I think, be inspirational, too. This garden, designed for Chaumont 2000, surrounds a circular pond with a decking path. Between the path and the surrounding hedge there was an extraordinary "planting" of folded metal.

sculpture and ornament

When it comes to sculpture and ornament, personal taste becomes critical. Both modern and traditional sculpture can be expensive – but need not be so. It is just a shape that is required, a manmade shape that contrasts with, complements, or terminates a view.

Scale is almost more important than content in making your selection. We usually end up with objects that are too small (smaller is cheaper). Not just size but mass, too, is vital – anything too "thin" simply disappears when seen from a distance.

Even taking into account the vagaries of personal taste, the choice available now makes it increasingly easy to find affordable sculptural features for the small garden.

Remember that these features will be seen through winter, too. Your sculptures will need some solidity when they are seen against bare plant stems.

"Try to stick to one material and relate it to the surface on which the objects sit."

The top of the urn was removed one night and not found again – but the car we assumed was used for the getaway was found abandoned with a bent rear axle – which nearly compensated for the loss of the stone urn!

Occasionally, traditional statuary in a modern setting looks wonderful, as can a modern piece in a more traditional one. Too many shock tactics can unsettle a garden, however.

Some of the nicest pieces to punctuate a garden, I believe, can be bought in secondhand masonry yards. Often they are not expensive and even have a touch of humor about them.

Pots and containers are often the cause of too much clutter. And yet if they are massed together on garden steps, or used to outline a pool in the Islamic way, they work. Perhaps we use containers made of too many different materials, with too many different types of plant fillings. The choice of material and size of pot that are now available seems almost limitless – throw in the odd urn and half barrel, and it is little wonder that the result can be rather indigestible.

Try to stick to one material and relate it to the surface on which the objects sit. Mood, too, will alter material. What is suitable for a swimming-pool terrace will not suit a cottage garden, for instance, and the grander period house will be different from the urban backlot garden.

I still think terracotta takes a lot of beating – though there are some clay colors that are less sympathetic than others. And terracotta pot shapes are getting simpler too. (I am not a great lover of swags over everything.) It is preferable to use large rather than small pots, because they do not dry out so quickly.

I have never seen anything wrong with concrete pots either. Once weathered they look fine to me when well planted. And this is the crunch. It is the planting that makes the pot. The odd oil jar can stand on its own as a sculptural piece, but most others need a really full planting, I believe – which happens naturally by the end of summer. I love half-barrels, too, which I think work well in most situations. You will need to keep them stained however, and damp – or the wood shrinks.

classical elements

LEFT It's the scale and silhouette of this eighteenth-century urn that creates the sense of drama in this parkland setting. The amount of surface decoration is of little importance until you get up close.
TOP Even in a smaller town garden, a small feature will still not make an impression from a distance. But by repetition, as here, with several containers, you can bring a kind of geometry to it, reinforcing the garden layout. This design is by Christopher Bradley-Hole.

containers

It is becoming more common for people to be more adventurous, not only with their choice of containers, but with the way they are planted, too.

One large container, well planted, can be most attractive. We tend to have too many, or to leave the pot and plant just as we bought them, which often means the plant just dries out and dies anyway!

The interesting thing about containers is not the material from which they are made, but how you use them. Positioned singly the pot (it doesn't necessarily need a plant) becomes a sculptural feature. Pots used repetitively become part of the overall design. Repetition can look good in the smaller garden, avoiding the all-too-familiar cluttered look.

What often happens is that we fall between two stools – we allow the plant to be more important than its container, and then mix up the types of container as well. There can be a happy medium – so long as the overall style is consistent. Whatever you do, decide upon one look, and go for it.

> *"Wooden furniture...although often expensive, is durable and has a lovely permanence about it."*

American friends turn up their noses at barrels, which they believe are on a par with pink flamingoes – we would think gnomes, I suppose. I love Versailles-type square planting boxes, which suit the current passion for topiary admirably.

Increasingly, I see metal containers being used. I can't believe that they do not get very hot and dry out rather quickly. But their effect is crisp and sharp – just right for that fashionable city terrace.

I do not have any trouble with fiberglass, although I might question its strength. Reconstituted stone for pots looks fine to me as well, in a stone setting, as of course does stone itself.

Probably a table and chairs for eating out provide the most functional of our fixtures outside. For myself, comfort should be the priority – and a fitness for the style of your garden. I have a green plastic table and chairs on my terrace. They have clean and simple lines, are easy to clean, and light to move around. I can stack them away in winter, too. But plastic is not considered very chic. I find this nonsensical – it all depends on the setting.

Wooden furniture is, I suppose, my next favorite. Although often expensive, it is durable and has a lovely permanence about it. I find nothing wrong in an unpretentious situation with a pine table and chairs for outside use, and they create a pleasant homey effect.

But homey effects and comforts seem far removed from many people's aspirations for their garden, and they prefer expensive metal furniture. If it is aluminum, and light to move around, I approve. I do not like heavy metal of any sort. There is something very organic about a garden in summer, and it is important to select materials to enhance and complement it.

Much of the furniture I see seems to be made for designers on city terraces. Although there is nothing wrong with this, city usage is very different from weekend or evening use in a more rural situation. In a place surrounded by urban buildings, the organic look is probably out of keeping anyway. So go for shape and clean lines in your urban furnishings and contrast them with strong architectural planting.

terrace furniture

TOP An American colonial setting into which traditional wooden garden furniture fits well.
RIGHT Slatted furniture looks stylish on a decked terrace in this garden by Andrew Duff. Notice the picture on the wall – protected by a preservative. This picture transforms the terrace into a garden room.

traditional garden furniture

The type of furniture you choose for your garden has as much to do with personal preference as it has to do with your garden style and layout. Comfort, too, is important. When placing furniture in a garden setting, your choice of materials should be sensitive to the environment. If your terrace is an extension of your internal living space, try to create a visual link between the furniture styles inside and out. I also think it is important that single garden chairs or sun loungers should create pleasing shapes in the landscape in their own right – they should be seen from a distance almost as a piece of sculpture.

modern garden furniture

With few exceptions, modern garden furniture has more to do with appearance than with comfort. On a stylish urban terrace, relaxation may not be the key concern. The furniture is often only suggestive, prompting those caught up in the frantic pace of city life to think "How lovely it would be to spend some time relaxing outside!" In an urban context, the shape of the furniture becomes more important. The material from which it is made need not be natural – it can be industrial stainless steel or fiberglass instead. The sculptural quality of the furniture is paramount, particularly if it is combined with modern plant containers or a contemporary garden ornament.

"My current fad is the painting of wooden furniture dark blue, which I think highlights the bench as an object in its own right..."

I would select furniture for sunbathing and relaxing using similar criteria. Make sure your garden terrace is large enough to accommodate the necessary furniture, and opt for comfort over style every time. It is more practical to use either a dark or patterned fabric for chair cushions and coverings as it will help hide inevitable marks or stains in this outdoor location.

Other furniture in a garden will include the bench seat, which will be a permanent fixture, and often provides a focal point within the layout. Make sure your choice is "in style" with your garden. My current fad is the painting of wooden furniture dark blue, which I think highlights the bench as an object in its own right (where natural wood seems to recede), and complements my choice of flower and foliage colors.

When writing of colors, a new element within the fixtures and fittings category is the large umbrella, which when open becomes almost a structure. They come in various colors and should complement your furniture. (Incidentally, they look wonderful with the colored-tile areas of a swimming pool.)

garden features

LEFT To make the most of an individual tree, put a seat around it, allowing lots of space for the tree to expand. It both anchors the tree to its site and makes a positive statement – "rest here," it says. Think about the area below the seat, which will be in the shade. Consider planting small shade-loving ferns.
TOP I've painted much of the furniture in my own garden this blue color, which gives a crisp look throughout, and blends well with plant material.

Talking structures again, I should mention balustrades and finials at this point. A balustrade can add a classical touch, but too much becomes pretentious. When contemplating this architectural feature you can find balustrades in stone, concrete, or reconstituted stone, and in various subtle colors to match a local stone – so do some research before making your selection. It is available in various sizes, and will, of course, need solid piers at intervals to support it. Finial balls as well as bases can give a lift to a garden, although I prefer the ball and no base. These are decorative elements, which if overdone can be a bit much – but add just the right "full stop" at times.

Other decorative elements within the garden might include wrought-iron screens and/or light fixtures. Very beautiful wrought-iron screens look wonderful supported on massive piers within old walls. But without the structural support, they can look heavy. Newer, finer wrought iron on the other hand can look too flimsy. But increasingly modern ironwork is available, which has enough substance without being too heavy.

It is better not to see light fixtures, and where possible always up-light, because a light placed high at night creates shadows that can be as dangerous as unseen obstacles. Consider safety factors when installing lighting. Run cables along the path edge so you know where they are, and make sure all external sockets have a cap so they can't be tampered with.

The subject of lighting a garden is quite a specialized art in itself. In the clement summer months of our British climate, we have daylight until quite late anyway – and then there are lights from the windows of the house. Yes, the occasional tree can be up-lit, but the huge panoply of fixtures available for this are excessive. In a warmer climate, where darkness comes earlier, but where it is still wonderful to be outside, subtle lighting can enhance the terrace for eating, for working over the barbeque, or for the swimming pool and the path leading to it.

You will need to think about lighting requirements when you are first planning your garden. Lay main cables to the key points when constructing your garden. Then get a specialized lighting expert to show you what can be done to enhance the special features of your garden once the garden is established, at a later date.

Always link style to location. If you live by the sea, for example, is the seashore sandy or pebbly? Is there a dune landscape? Or do you live near fresh water? If so, is it a calm inland lake or is it a torrent through your garden? Each type of water is appropriate to its own landscape, and your styling should reflect this.

Trying to create the garden style of another culture is difficult, since the light and climate are so different. I will never be satisfied with another Western version of a Japanese garden again – having seen some of the originals. Having said that, ideas can be transposed – and that's the secret.

I hope that by reading my thoughts on garden design, formulated from the years I have spent running my own design practice and school for garden design students, that you will have gained the confidence and the expert knowledge to conceive and implement your own garden layout.

lighting garden features

TOP I'm all for subtle lighting outside – these simple up-lighters just bring to life the tubs between them and the planting on the wall beyond.

RIGHT White oleander in tubs with candlelight upon a Riviera terrace – how romantic. Lighting is kept to a minimum in this beautiful garden by Claus Shiner.

lighting

I find this rather a thorny subject, since I seldom see lighting done well on a domestic scale. When it is, the effect can be magical – but a good result is usually the result of less light rather than more. You do need something to light up a wonderful tree or a piece of statuary, or to light a deep blue pool from underwater.

I also think you need warm evenings to sit out and enjoy your lighting, although a well-lit snowy scene from a snug interior has great charm as well.

index

Page references in **bold** indicate illustrations and/or their captions.

acknowledgements

Author's acknowledgements
I would like to acknowledge my associate Michael Neve and all my staff at Denmans, in particular Emma Sollom. I would also like to thank Nada Jennet for access to her photographs.

In preparation of this book, I would like to thank Colin Walton and Bella Pringle of Walton and Pringle and Melanie Watson for picture research.

Publisher's acknowledgements
Dorling Kindersley would like to thank the indexer Dawn Butcher; Michael Axworthy, and Susie Behar for editorial assitance; Alison Lotinga for design advice.

Illustrations
Richard Lee

Photographic credits
The publishers would like to thank the following photographers, garden owners, and garden designers.
T=top **L**=left **R**=right **C**=center **B**=below **LOC**=Location **DES**=Designer

1 Andrew Lawson **LOC** Denmans, East Sussex **DES** John Brookes
2 Steven Wooster
3 Andrew Lawson **LOC** Denmans, East Sussex **DES** John Brookes
4 T John Brookes **DES** Martha Schwartz
4 C Garden Picture Library / Mark Bolton
4 B Jerry Harpur **DES** Steve Martino, Phoenix, Arizona, USA
6 Andrew Lawson **LOC** Denmans, East Sussex **DES** John Brookes
9 Robert Harding / Geoff Renner
10 RIBA Library Drawings Collection, London
11 John Brookes
12 Hugh Palmer **LOC** Château de Vaux-le-Vicomte, France
13, 14 John Brookes
15 Andrew Lawson **DES** David Hicks
16 John Brookes
17 Garden Picture Library / Clay Perry **LOC** Hestercombe, Somerset **DES** Gertrude Jekyll & Edwin Lutyens
18 Peter Anderson **LOC** El Novillero, San Francisco, California, USA **DES** Thomas Church
19 Jeffrey Howe
20 Marijke Heuff **DES** Jacques Wirtz, Belgium
21 John Brookes **LOC** Hestercombe, Somerset **DES** Gertrude Jekyll
22 Garden Picture Library / John Glover **LOC** Munstead Wood, Surrey **DES** Gertrude Jekyll
23 Hugh Palmer **LOC** Filkins **DES** Brenda Colvin
24 John Brookes
25 Colin Walton **LOC** Framfield, East Sussex
26 John Brookes **DES** Isabelle C. Greene
27 Garden Picture Library / Ron Sutherland **LOC** RHS Chelsea 2000, Daily Telegraph Garden **DES** Christopher Bradley-Hole
28 T Garden Picture Library / Christopher Gallagher
28 C John Brookes
28 B Skyscan Photolibrary
29 T, B Woodfall Wild Images / David Woodfall
29 C Woodfall Wild Images / Bill Coster
30 Jerry Harpur **DES** P. Clifford Miller, Lake Forest, Illinois, USA
33 Skyscan/Jason Hawkes Library
34 T Woodfall Wild Images / David Woodfall
34 C, B Colin Walton
35 TR, TL, BR Colin Walton
35 C Woodfall Wild Images / Jeremy Woodhouse
35 BL Skyscan/Nick Hanna
36 Skyscan Photolibrary
37 T Jerry Harpur
38 T Skyscan Photolibrary
38 B Robert Harding / Louise Murray
39 TR Woodfall Wild Images / David Woodfall
39 TL Woodfall Wild Images / M. Biancarelli
39 BR Skyscan/Brian Lea
39 BL Skyscan Photolibrary
40 T John Brookes
40 L Steven Wooster **LOC** Thrumm Garden, Napier, New Zealand
41 Peter Anderson **LOC** Tucson, AZ **DES** Richard Wogisch
42 T Woodfall Wild Images / David Woodfall
42 B Garden Picture Library / Nick Meers
44 T Garden Picture Library / Kathy Charlton
44 L Ecoscene / Tony Page
45 Clive Nichols
46 B, 47 TL Colin Walton
46 T, 47 BR, BL John Brookes
47 TR Nick Ivins
48 David Markson **LOC** Clos du Peyonnet, France
49 T Jerry Harpur **LOC** La Casella, Opio, France
49 R John Brookes
50 David Markson **LOC** Pashley Manor, East Sussex
51 John Brookes
52 Andrew Lawson **DES** Penelope Hobhouse
53 T Jerry Harpur **DES** Juan Grimm, Santiago, Chile
53 R, 54 T John Brookes
54 B Garden Exposures Photo Library (Andrea Jones) **COURTESY** The Monteiro Estate, Brazil **DES** Roberto Burle Marx
56 T Colin Walton
56 B Woodfall Wild Images / Rob Blayers
57 T Woodfall Wild Images / David Woodfall
57 C, B Woodfall Wild Images / Ted Mead
58 Clive Nichols
60 R Andrew Lawson **LOC** Denmans, East Sussex **DES** John Brookes
60 L Colin Walton
61 Garden Picture Library / John Ferro Sims
62 T, C Clive Nichols
62 B Marcus Harpur
63 TR Colin Walton
63 TL Nicola Browne
63 BR Jerry Harpur
63 BL Jonathan Buckley **LOC** Upper Mill Cottage, Kent **DES** David & Mavis Seeney
64 Vivian Russell
67 Sofia Brignone from *The Modern Garden* by Jane Brown, published by Thames & Hudson Ltd. London. pp 42-43, 47 **ARCHITECT** Gabriel Guevrékian
68 B David Markson
68 T, 69 TL Derek Harris
69 TR Clive Streeter
69 BR John Brookes
69 BL Jo Whitworth **LOC** RHS Chelsea **DES** A. Lennox Boyd
70 Garden Picture Library / Clive Boursnell **LOC** Sutton Place, Surrey **DES** Geoffrey Jellicoe
71 Paul Raftery/www.arcaid.co.uk **LOC** Villa Savoye, France **ARCHITECT** Le Corbusier

72 T Phillips Collection, Washington DC Bridgeman Art Library **LOC** Trendine, Cornwall, December 1947 **ARTIST** Ben Nicholson

72 C Architects Journal **LOC** St Ann's Hill, Chertsey, Surrey **DES** Raymond McGrath & Christopher Tunnard

73 John Brookes **DES** Martha Schwartz

74 CL Architecural Review **LOC** Bentley Wood, Halland, Sussex, UK **DES** Serge Chermayeff & Christopher Tunnard

74 BL Henry Moore Foundation

75 Jerry Harpur **DES** Garret Eckbo, San Francisco, CA

76 T Haruyoshi Ono **LOC** Farenda Marambaia Correas, RJ, Brazil **DES** Roberto Burle Marx

76 B Colin Walton **LOC** North America

78 T Nicola Browne **LOC** Marina Linear Park **DES** Martha Schwartz

78 B Jerry Harpur **DES** Steve Martino, Phoenix, AZ

79 TR Garden Exposures Photo Library (Andrea Jones) **LOC** Galloway labyrinth, Scotland **DES** Jim Buchanan

79 TL John Brookes **LOC** Sonoma, CA **DES** Thomas Church

79 BR Jonathan Buckley **LOC** Westwood Park, London **DES** Jackie McLaren

79 BL Jo Whitworth **LOC** Feng Shui Garden, RHS Hampton Court **DES** Pamela Woods

80 T Modest Herwig

80 C John Edward Linden/www.arcaid.co.uk **LOC** Andy Fletcher House, Marlow, Bucks **ARCH** John Newton

80 B View / Chris Gascoigne **ARCH** Nicholas Burwell

84 CL, 84 BL John Brookes **LOC** Stuart Jackman & Anne-Marie Bulat, London **DES** John Brookes

86-89 John Brookes

90 Garden Picture Library / John Ferro Sims **LOC** Wales

93 Philippe Perdereau **DES** Jacques Wirtz

95 John Heseltine **LOC** Piemonte Vineyards, Asti, Italy

96 T John Brookes

96 B Garden Picture Library / Howard Rice

97 TR Hugh Palmer **LOC** Hatfield House, Herts

97 TL John Brookes

97 BR Mark Bolton **LOC** Laurent Perrier Garden RHS Chelsea **DES** Tom Stuart Smith

97 BL John Brookes

99 Aaron Kiley **LOC** Miller House, Columbus, OH **DES** Dan Kiley, **SCULPTURE** Henry Moore

100 T Philippe Perdereau

100 C Jerry Harpur **DES** Steve Martino, Phoenix, AZ

100 B Woodfall Wild Images / David Woodfall

101 TR John Brookes

101 TL Woodfall Wild Images / M. Biancarelli

101 BR Clive Streeter

101 BL Jerry Harpur **LOC** Tintinhull House Garden, Somerset **DES** Penelope Hobhouse

102 Steven Wooster

104 Marijke Heuff **DES** Jacques Wirtz, Belgium

105 Philippe Perdereau **DES** Jacques Wirtz

106 Philippe Perdereau **DES** Arend Jan van der Horst

108 T Jonathan Buckley **LOC** Petherton Rd, London, **DES** Declan Buckley

108 B Jo Whitworth **LOC** Oxford

109 TR John Brookes

109 TL Jerry Harpur **DES** Dan Kiley, Boston, MA

109 B Jonathan Buckley **LOC** Ketley's, East Sussex **DES** Helen Yemm

111 John Brookes **LOC** Gardeners World Garden, Birmingham

112 Clive Nichols **DES** Vic Shanley

115 Nicola Browne **DES** Ros Palmer

116-117 John Brookes

118 T Jerry Harpur **DES** P. Hobhouse & A. Pfeiffer

118 B Steven Wooster **LOC** Milton Winery, New Zealand

119 T Nicola Browne **DES** Veronique Maria

119 B Jonathan Buckley **LOC** The Evening Standard garden, RHS Chelsea **DES** Xa Tollemarche

121 John Brookes **LOC** Eccleston Manor

122 Clive Nichols **LOC** Austin TX **DES** Gordon White

124 Nicola Browne **DES** Ulf Nordfjell

125 B John Brookes

126 T Steven Wooster **LOC** The Horton Garden, Auckland, New Zealand

126 B John Heseltine

127 TR John Brookes

127 TL Colin Walton **LOC** Reales Alcazares, Seville, Spain

127 BR John Heseltine

127 BL Colin Walton **DES** Mr. & Mrs. Jeremy Clark

128-129 John Brookes

130 L Garden Picture Library / Alec Scaresbrook **LOC** RHS Chelsea 1998 **DES** Bunny Guinness & Wyevale Design Team

131 Marianne Majerus

132 Jerry Harpur **DES** Juan Grimm, Santiago, Chile

133 T Clive Streeter

134 T David Glomb **DES** Marcello Villano

134 C Jo Whitworth **LOC** Manoir aux Quat' Saisons, Oxfordshire

134 B Colin Walton **DES** Mr. and Mrs. Mike Dade

135 TR Clive Nichols **DES** Avant Gardener

135 TL Clive Streeter

135 CR Modest Herwig **LOC** Van Gent family, Holland **DES** Roelie de Weerd, Holland **TEL** +31 35 526 39 82

135 BR Jo Whitworth Loc Fovant Hut, Wiltshire **DES** Christina Oates together with her husband Nigel. The garden is open to the public **TEL** 01722 714756 **WEB** www.secretgardendesigns.co.uk

135 BL Nada Jennet **DES** Preben Jacobsen

136 T Colin Walton **LOC** Cabbages and Kings, Wilderness Farm, Hadlow Down, East Sussex. **TEL** 01825 830552 **WEB** www.ckings.co.uk
The Cabbages and Kings garden, subtitled "The Centre for Garden Design" was devised to explain how garden design principles work in practice. A series of interlocking spaces lead out to to glorious views, each relating to the buildings and to the landscape to which they belong. **DES** Ryl Nowell

136 C John Brookes

138 T David Glomb **DES** Marcello Villano

138 B Jonathan Buckley

139 TR Modest Herwig **LOC** Fleurig Flowershow, Barneveld, Holland **DES** Meratus Hoveniers

139 TL Garden Picture Library / Mayer / Le Scanff **LOC** Festival de Jardins de Chaumont, France

139 CR Jerry Harpur **DES** Isabelle Greene, Santa Barbara, CA

139 CL Alan Weintraub / www.arcaid.co.uk **LOC** Beyer House, Malibu, CA **ARCH** John Lautner

139 B John Heseltine

140 Henk Dijkman **LOC** Holland **DES** Mein Ruys

141 John Heseltine

142-145 John Brookes

146 Peter Anderson **LOC** Davis Residence, El Paso, Texas **DES** Martha Schwartz

149 Alan Weintraub / www.arcaid.co.uk **LOC** Ganymede House, Del Dios, CA

150 T John Brookes **LOC** Fondation Maeght

151 ArtArchive

152 T Jerry Harpur **DES** Chris Rosmini, Los Angeles, CA

152 B Garden Picture Library / Gil Hanly

153 TR John Brookes

153 TL Jerry Harpur **DES** Sonny Garcia, San Francisco, CA

153 B Jerry Harpur **DES** Juan Grimm, Santiago, Chile

154 T Alan Weintraub **WEB** www.arcaid.co.uk **LOC** Segel House, Malibu, CA **ARCH** John Lautner

154 B Jerry Harpur **DES** Luciano Giubbilei, London

155 TR Jerry Harpur **DES** Steve Martino, Phoenix, AZ

155 TL Jerry Harpur **DES** Luciano Giubbilei, London

155 B John Brookes

157 Jerry Harpur **DES** Isabelle Greene, Santa Barbara

158 T Jerry Harpur **DES** Juan Grimm, Santiago, Chile

158 B Nicola Browne **DES** Steve Martino

159 TR John Brookes

159 TL Nicola Browne **DES** Christopher Bradley-Hole

159 BR Jerry Harpur **DES** Martha Schwartz, Cambridge, MA

159 BL John Brookes

160 Jerry Harpur **DES** Luciano Giubbilei, London

161 B John Brookes

162 T Nicola Browne **DES** Martha Schwartz

162 B Jerry Harpur **DES** Jeff Mendoza, New York City

163 T Jerry Harpur **LOC** Buenos Aires, Argentina **DES** Pratial Gutierrez, BA, Argentina

163 BR Peter Anderson **LOC** Tucson, AZ **DES** Philip Van Wyck

163 BL ArtArchive

164 T Jerry Harpur **DES** Fred Mengoni, New York City

164 L Jerry Harpur **LOC** Japanese Garden, Portland, OR

166 T Jerry Harpur **DES** Jenny Jones, Highwater Design, Isle of Wight

166 C Clive Nichols **LOC** Hedens Lustgard, Sweden **DES** Ulf Nordfjell

166 B Modest Herwig **LOC** Gardens of Appeltern, Appeltern, Holland **TEL** +31 487 541 732 **WEB** www.appeltern.nl **DES** Henk Weijers, Holland **TEL** +31 23 531 78 01

167 TR Mark Bolton

167 TL Clive Nichols **DES** Paul Thompson & Trevyn McDowell

167 BR Jo Whitworth **LOC** Bosvigo House, Cornwall

167 BL Jerry Harpur **LOC** Kyoto Japan **DES** Marc Peter Keane

168-170 John Brookes

170 B Mark Bolton **LOC** RHS Chelsea 2000 (Blue Circle garden)

171 T Modest Herwig **LOC** Weerman family, Holland **DES** Henk Weijers, Holland. **TEL** +31 23 531 78 01

171 BR Jonathan Buckley **LOC** A Real Japanese Garden (The Daily Telegraph) RHS Chelsea 2001 **DES** Professor Masao Fukuhara

171 BL John Brookes

172 T Nicola Browne **DES** David & Judy Drew

172 B Jonathan Buckley **LOC** A Brush with the Past RHS Chelsea 2001 **DES** Heath End Gardening Club

173 T Andrew Duff

173 CR Rob Whitworth **LOC** Wyken Hall, Suffolk

173 CL Colin Walton

173 BR Jo Whitworth **LOC** Frith Hill, West Sussex

173 BL Jonathan Buckley

174 Jerry Harpur

177-8 Modest Herwig

179 View / Peter Cook **LOC** Fowler House, London **ARCH** Jestico & Whiles

180 T Nicola Browne **DES** Steve Martino

180 C John Heseltine

180 B Jonathan Buckley **LOC** East Ruston Old Vicarage, Norfolk **DES** Alan Gray & Graham Robeson

181 TR Nicola Browne **DES** Lodewijk Baljon

181 TL View / Philip Bier **ARCHITECT** Foster & Partners

181 BR Peter Anderson **LOC** Tucson, AZ **DES** Philip Van Wyck

181 BL Jerry Harpur **DES** Isabelle Greene, Santa Barbara, CA

183 Colin Walton **DES** Mr. and Mrs. Mike Dade

184 T Garden Picture Library / Erika Craddock **LOC** Le Bois des Moutiers, France **DES** Gertrude Jekyll

184 C Henk Dijkman **DES** Henk Weijers

184 B John Brookes

185 TR Melanie Watson

185 TL Peter Anderson **LOC** Tucson, AZ **DES** Richard Wogisch

185 BR Peter Anderson **LOC** Hodges Barn, Gloucestershire

185 BL Jonathan Buckley **LOC** Great Dixter, East Sussex **DES** Christopher Lloyd

186 T Edifice / Gillian Darley **ARCHITECTS** Aldingham & Craig

186 B View / Dennis Gilbert **LOC** Cluny Park, Singapore

ARCHITECTS KNTA Architects
188 Clive Nichols **LOC** RHS Chelsea 1998 **DES** Blakedown Landscapes
191 Jonathan Buckley
192 Jonathan Buckley **LOC** Merton Hall Road, London **DES** Gay Wilson
193 BR John Brookes
194 T Andrew Lawson **LOC** Denmans, East Sussex **DES** John Brookes
194 C John Brookes **LOC** Villa Noailles, Toulon, France
194 B Colin Walton **DES** Walton & Flett
195 T John Heseltine
195 BR John Brookes
195 BL Garden Picture Library / Mark Bolton
196 Jerry Harpur **LOC** Folly Farm, Berkshire
197 T Garden Picture Library / Jiri Merz
197 R Jerry Harpur **LOC** Dumbarton Oaks, Washington DC
198 T Modest Herwig **LOC** Steenbakkers family, Holland **DES** Arend-Jan van der Horst, Holland **TEL** +31 113 567 223
198 C Derek Harris
198 B Colin Walton **DES** Mr. & Mrs. Steve Crosby
199 TR Jo Whitworth **LOC** RHS Hampton Court 2000 **DES** Land Art
199 TL John Brookes
199 CL Modest Herwig **LOC** Fleurig Flowershow, Barneveld, Holland
199 BR Jo Whitworth **LOC** Barleywood, Hampshire **DES** Alan Titchmarsh
199 BL Colin Walton
200 Marianne Majerus **DES** Michele Osborne
201 T Colin Walton **LOC** Monaco, France
201 R Steven Wooster **LOC** Ohinetahi, New Zealand
202 T David Markson **LOC** Rotherfield Cottage, East Sussex
202 C Andrew Duff
202 B Colin Walton
203 TR David Glomb **DES** Peter Gluck
203 TL Jo Whitworth **LOC** Bosvigo House, Cornwall
203 CR John Brookes **LOC** RHS Hampton Court 2000 **DES** JWP Landscape Architects
203 CL Rob Whitworth
203 BR Jonathan Buckley **LOC** Merton Hall Road, London **DES** Gay Wilson
203 BL Andrew Duff
204 T Jerry Harpur **DES** Juan Grimm, Santiago, Chile
204 L Jerry Harpur **DES** Oehme & Van Sweden, Washington DC
205 John Brookes
206 T Jonathan Buckley **LOC** Loddon Road, Reading, Berkshire **DES** Janet Bonney
206 C Rob Whitworth **LOC** Wyken Hall, Suffolk
206 B Jonathan Buckley **LOC** Lyndhurst Square, London **DES** Josephine Picket-Baker
207 T Modest Herwig **LOC** Elings family, Holland **DES** Jacqueline van der Kloet, Holland **TEL** +31 294 41 44 86
207 BR Jerry Harpur **LOC** Kyoto, Japan
207 BL Jerry Harpur **DES** Marc Peter Keane, Kyoto, Japan
208 T Andrew Lawson **LOC** Denmans, E. Sussex **DES** John Brookes
208 L Steven Wooster **LOC** "La Main Coulante" Chaumont 2001, France **DES** Gardeners of the Conservatory
209 Henk Dijkman
210 T John Brookes
210 L Jo Whitworth **LOC** Fovant Hut, Wiltshire see picture credit **135 BR** for more details
211 John Brookes
212 T Mark Bolton **LOC** Hamblyns Coombe, Devon Sculptures **DES** Bridget McCrum
212 C Jonathan Buckley **LOC** A Fisherman's Retreat RHS Chelsea 2001 **DES** Emsworth Horticultural Society
212 B Jo Whitworth **LOC** RHS Hampton Court 1999 **DES** Anglo Aquarian Plants
213 TR Clive Nichols **LOC** Beth Chatto Garden, Essex

DES Beth Chatto
213 TL Nicola Browne **DES** Faith Oquma
213 CL Garden Picture Library / Ron Sutherland **DES** Anthony Paul
213 BR Neil Sutherland
213 BL Modest Herwig **LOC** De Heerenhof, Maastricht, Holland **TEL** +31 43 408 48 00 **WEB** www.heerenhof.nl
214 B Clive Nichols **LOC** Living Sculpture Garden RHS Chelsea 2000 (The Daily Telegraph / RF Hotels) **DES** Christopher Bradley Hole
215 T John Brookes
216 T Garden Picture Library / Ron Sutherland **DES** Anthony Paul
216 B Nicola Browne **DES** Ros Palmer
217 Garden Picture Library / Ron Sutherland **DES** Anthony Paul
218 T Garden Picture Library / Ron Sutherland **DES** Anthony Paul
218 B Nicola Browne **DES** Avant Gardener
219 TR John Brookes **LOC** RHS Chelsea 2000 **DES** Christopher Bradley-Hole
219 TL Peter Anderson **LOC** El Novillero, San Francisco, CA **DES** Thomas Church
219 C Jonathan Buckley **LOC** The Laurent-Perrier Harpers & Queen Garden RHS Chelsea 2001 **DES** Tom Stuart Smith **PLANTING** Jinny Blom
219 BR Jo Whitworth **LOC** RHS Chelsea 2000 **DES** Richard Sneesby
219 BL Nicola Browne **LOC** Gardeners World Garden, Birmingham **DES** John Brookes
220 T Modest Herwig **LOC** Weerman family, Holland **DES** Henk Weijers, Holland. **TEL** +31 23 531 78 01
220 B Jerry Harpur **DES** Steve Martino, Phoenix, Arizona
221 T David Glomb **DES** Huell Howser
221 CR Nicola Browne **DES** Bonita Baralitus
221 CL John Brookes
221 BR Jonathan Buckley **LOC** The Tastevin Garden RHS Chelsea 2001 **DES** Pickard School of Design
221 BL Woodfall Wild Images / David Woodfall
222 Garden Picture Library / Henk Dijkman
225 John Brookes
226 John Brookes
227 Jonathan Buckley **LOC** Merton Hall Road, London **DES** Gay Wilson
228 T John Brookes
228 C John Heseltine
228 B Paul David Adams
229 TR Jo Whitworth **LOC** Fovant Hut, Wiltshire see picture credit **135 BR** for more details
229 TL John Heseltine
229 BR Jerry Harpur **DES** Jonathan Turner, London
229 BL Modest Herwig
230 John Heseltine
231 John Brookes
232 T Garden Picture Library / Ron Sutherland **DES** Anthony Paul
232 B Mark Bolton **LOC** The Old Chapel, Chalfield, Glos
233 TR John Heseltine
233 TL Neil Sutherland
233 BR John Brookes
233 BL Derek Harris
234 Jerry Harpur **DES** Luciano Giubbilei, London
235 Jonathan Buckley **LOC** Ketley's, East Sussex **DES** Helen Yemm
236 T Marianne Majerus **LOC** RHS Chelsea 2000 **DES** Brita von Schoenaich
236 L John Brookes **LOC** Holland Garden, Sussex **DES** John Brookes
237 Nicola Browne **DES** Martha Schwartz
238 T Peter Anderson **LOC** San Francisco, CA **DES** Jack Chandler
238 B Modest Herwig **LOC** Winterink family, Holland

239 TR Modest Herwig **LOC** Weerman family, Holland **DES** Henk Weijers, Holland **TEL** +31 23 531 78 01
239 TL Jo Whitworth **LOC** Fovant Hut, Wiltshire see picture credit **135 BR** for more details
239 B Jerry Harpur **LOC** Kyoto, Japan
240 Henk Dijkman
241 T Jerry Harpur **DES** Isabelle Greene, Santa Barbara, CA
241 R Nicola Browne **DES** Ganna Walska Lotusland
242 T Nicola Browne **DES** Andy Sturgeon
242 B Jo Whitworth **DES** Longstock Park Nursery, Hampshire
243 TR Modest Herwig **LOC** Museum of American Art, Giverny, France
243 TL Garden Picture Library / Erika Craddock **DES** Gertrude Jekyll and Edwin Lutyens
243 B Jerry Harpur **DES** Chris Rosmini, Los Angeles, CA
244 TR John Brookes
245 Clive Streeter
246 T Modest Herwig **LOC** Gardens of Appeltern, Holland **DES** Meneer Vermeer Gardens **TEL** +31 226 39 39 20
246 B Paul David Adams
247 TR Steven Wooster **LOC** Titoki Point, New Zealand
247 TL John Brookes
247 CR Modest Herwig **LOC** Rademaker family, Holland
247 CL Colin Walton
247 BR Mark Bolton **LOC** RHS Chelsea 2000 (Blue Circle Garden)
247 BL Colin Walton **LOC** Benefice Farm, Cheshire
247 BC Jonathan Buckley **LOC** Culverden Road, London **DES** Nick Ryan
248 Garden Picture Library / Steven Wooster
251 Jonathan Buckley **LOC** Ketley's, East Sussex **DES** Helen Yemm
252 Hugh Palmer **LOC** Filkins **DES** Brenda Colvin
253 B Hugh Palmer **LOC** St. Catherine's College, Oxford **DES** Arne Jacobsen
254 T Derek Harris
254 C Marijke Heuff
254 B Steven Wooster **LOC** Thijsse Park, Holland
255 TR Juliette Wade **LOC** The Old Vicarage, East Ruston, Norfolk **DES** Alan Gray & Graham Robeson
255 TL Jerry Harpur **LOC** Villa Gamberaia, Florence, Italy
255 BR Jerry Harpur **DES** Frank Cabot, Canada
255 BL Philippe Perdereau **DES** Jacques Wirtz
256 Henk Dijkman **DES** Jacques Wirtz
257 T Jonathan Buckley **LOC** Great Dixter, East Sussex **DES** Christopher Lloyd
258 T Steven Wooster
258 B Nicola Browne **DES** Piet Oudolf
259 TR Steven Wooster **LOC** Lea Dunster's Garden, Akaroa, New Zealand
259 TL Mark Bolton **LOC** Urn Cottage, Gloucestershire
259 BR Mark Bolton
259 BL Colin Walton
260 T John Brookes
260 B Garden Exposures Photo Library (Andrea Jones) **DES** Oehme & Van Sweden
262 T Jerry Harpur **DES** Steve Martino, Phoenix, AZ
262 B Rob Whitworth **LOC** RHS Hampton Court 2000 (Active Mind: Active Body) **DES** JWP Landscape Architects
263 TR Jo Whitworth **LOC** RHS Hampton Court 2000 **DES** Land Art
263 TL Nicola Browne **DES** Piet Oudolf
263 BR Jonathan Buckley **LOC** American Impressionists Garden, Giverny, France **DES** Mark Brown
263 BL Rob Whitworth **LOC** RHS Hampton Court 2000 (The Queen Victoria Hospital Burns Garden) **DES** Jeremy Salt & Roger Bullock
264 T John Brookes
265 Andrew Lawson **LOC** Westpark, Munich **DES** Rosemary Weisse
266 Steven Wooster **LOC** Briar Rose Cottage, Orinoco, New Zealand

267 T Peter Anderson **DES** Peter Anderson

267 John Brookes

268 Steven Wooster **LOC** Hadspen House Gardens, Somerset

269, 270 T Clive Nichols **DES** Ton Ter Linden

270 C Clive Nichols

270 B Clive Nichols **LOC** Hadspen House Gardens, Somerset

271 TR Andrew Lawson **DES** Penelope Hobhouse

271 TL Philippe Perdereau **DES** Ton Ter Linden

271 BR Jonathan Buckley **LOC** Waterperry Gardens, Oxford

271 BL Andrew Lawson **LOC** Tintinhull House, Somerset
DES Penelope Hobhouse

272 John Brookes **DES** Beth Chatto

273 Jerry Harpur **DES** Piet Oudolf, Holland for Green Farm Plants, Hants

274 T Garden Exposures Photo Library (Andrea Jones)
LOC Lady Farm, Somerset
COURTESY of Mr. & Mrs. M. Pearce

275 Clive Nichols **LOC** Lady Farm, Somerset

276-8 Andrew Lawson **LOC** Denmans, E. Sussex **DES** John Brookes

278 C Rob Whitworth **LOC** Lady Farm, Somerset

278 B Jonathan Buckley **LOC** Beth Chatto's Garden, Essex
DES Beth Chatto

279 TR Peter Anderson **LOC** Acres Wild Landscape and Garden Design, Billingshurst, West Sussex
DES Debbie Roberts & Ian Shaw

279 TL Garden Exposures Photo Library (Andrea Jones)
COURTESY Channel 4, Wild about the Garden

279 BR Peter Anderson **LOC** Acres Wild Landscape and Garden Design, Billingshurst, West Sussex
DES Debbie Roberts & Ian Shaw

279 BL John Brookes **LOC** Denmans, E. Sussex **DES** John Brookes

280 Nicola Browne **DES** Jinny Blom

281 Peter Anderson **LOC** Tucson, AZ **DES** Philip Van Wyck

282 T Peter Anderson **LOC** Tucson, AZ **DES** Philip Van Wyck

282 B Steven Wooster **LOC** Diana Firth's Garden, Auckland, New Zealand

283 T Steven Wooster **LOC** Jack Richard's Garden, Wainui Beach, New Zealand

283 B Steven Wooster **LOC** Wild lupine field, South Island, New Zealand

284 Jonathan Buckley **LOC** Ketley's, East Sussex **DES** Helen Yemm

285 Nicola Browne **DES** Laure Quonium

287 T Andrew Lawson **LOC** Denmans, E. Sussex **DES** John Brookes

287 R Steven Wooster **LOC** "La Main Coulante" Chaumont **2001**, France **DES** Gardeners of the Conservatory

288 T John Brookes

288 L Steven Wooster **LOC** The Isabella Plantation, Richmond Park, Surrey

290 T Nada Jennet **LOC** Sissinghurst, Kent **DES** Vita Sackville-West

290 B Steven Wooster **LOC** Beth Chatto Garden, Essex

291 T Garden Exposures Photo Library (Andrea Jones)
LOC Great Dixter, East Sussex **DES** Christopher Lloyd

291 BR Andrew Lawson **LOC** Denmans **DES** John Brookes

291 BL Nicola Browne **DES** Dan Pearson

293 Modest Herwig **LOC** Piet Oudolf's Garden, Hummelo, Holland **DES** Piet Oudolf

294 Garden Picture Library / Jerry Pavia

297 John Brookes **LOC** Denmans **DES** John Brookes

298 SkyScan Photolibrary

299 T Woodfall Wild Images / David Woodfall

300 T Jo Whitworth **LOC** Beth Chatto Garden, Essex
DES Beth Chatto

300 B Garden Picture Library / Steven Wooster **DES** Henk Weijers

301 T Steven Wooster **LOC** The RHS Gardens, Hyde Hall, Essex

301 B Neil Sutherland

302 Jo Whitworth **LOC** Wyken Hall, Suffolk

303 John Brookes **LOC** Denmans **DES** John Brookes

304 Woodfall Wild Images / David Woodfall

305 Jerry Harpur **DES** P Clifford Miller, Lake Forest, IL

306 Garden Picture Library / Mayer/Le Scanff **LOC** Les Jardins

de L'Imaginaire, Terrasson, France **DES** K Gustafson

307 Jerry Harpur

308 TR John Brookes

309 John Brookes **LOC** Holland Garden, Sussex **DES** John Brookes

310 T Modest Herwig **LOC** Rhulenhof Tuinen, Ottersum, Holland **TEL** +31 485 51 80 39
WEB www.rhulenhof.nl

310 B Jerry Harpur **DES** Richard Hartlage, Seattle, WA

311 TR Peter Anderson **LOC** Santa Barbara, CA
DES Isabelle Greene

311 TL Clive Nichols **LOC** Wollerton Old Hall, Shropshire

311 CR Derek Harris **LOC** RHS Hampton Court

311 CL Hugh Palmer **LOC** Casa de Pilatos, Seville, Spain

311 BR Jonathan Buckley **LOC** Southlands, Manchester
DES Maureen Sawyer

311 BL Jonathan Buckley **LOC** RHS Chelsea 2000 (Blue Circle garden) **DES** Carole Vincent

312 John Brookes

313 Jerry Harpur **DES** Steve Martino, Phoenix, AZ

314 Jerry Harpur **DES** John Douglas, Phoenix, AZ

315 CL John Brookes

316 T Henk Dijkman

316 C Nicola Browne **DES** Faith Oquma

316 B Clive Nichols **DES** Claire Mee

317 TR Clive Nichols **LOC** Hedens Lustgard, Sweden
DES Ulf Nordfjell

317 TL Modest Herwig **LOC** Rhulenhof Tuinen, Ottersum, Holland. **TEL** +31 485 51 80 39
WEB www.rhulenhof.nl **DES** Huub Kortekaas

317 BR John Brookes

317 BL Colin Walton **LOC** Fondation Ephrussi de Rothschild, Cap Ferrat, France

318 T Clive Nichols **LOC** San Francisco, CA
DES Christian Wright

318 L Jo Whitworth **LOC** Fovant Hut, Wiltshire see picture credit **135 BR** for more details

319 David Glomb **DES** Richard Corsini

320 T Alan Weintraub/www.arcaid.co.uk **ARCHITECT** John Lautner

320 C Peter Anderson **LOC** The Village Pond, San Francisco, CA
DES Thomas Church

320 B Peter Anderson **LOC** Santa Barbara, CA
DES Isabelle Greene

321 TR Nicola Browne **DES** Steve Martino

321 TL Peter Anderson **LOC** San Francisco, CA
DES Richard Wogisch

321 CR Jerry Harpur **LOC** Old Nectar' Stellenbosch, South Africa

321 CL Andrew Lawson **LOC** New Zealand **DES** Ted Smyth

321 BR Peter Anderson **LOC** Tucson, AZ
DES Philip Van Wyck

321 BL Peter Anderson **LOC** Hodges Barn, Gloucestershire

322 Garden Picture Library / Steven Wooster
SCULPTURE Pat Volk

325 Steven Wooster **LOC** "Mente la Menta?" Chaumont 2000, France **DES** Marco Antononi, Gianna Attiani, Roberto Capecci, Daniela Mongini & Rafaella Sini

326 T Steven Wooster **LOC** The O'Sullivan's Racing Stables Garden, New Zealand

326 B Steven Wooster

327 TR Philippe Perdereau **DES** Arend Jan van der Horst

327 TL John Brookes

327 BR Colin Walton **LOC** Denmans **DES** John Brookes, **SCULPTOR** Jim Partridge

327 BL Colin Walton **LOC** Denmans **DES** John Brookes, **SCULPTURE** Andrea Schulewitz

328 John Brookes **LOC** Petworth, West Sussex

329 Nicola Browne **DES** Christopher Bradley-Hole

330 T Nicola Browne

330 B Jerry Harpur **LOC** San Francisco, CA
DES Sonny Garcia, San Francisco, CA

331 TR Garden Exposures Photo Library (Andrea Jones)
LOC New York Botanical Gardens, New York City

331 TL Nicola Browne **DES** Ulf Nordfjell

331 BR Jonathan Buckley **LOC** Circ Contemporary Man's Garden RHS Chelsea **DES** Andy Sturgeon

331 BL Andrew Lawson **DES** Penelope Hobhouse

332 Garden Exposures Photo Library (Andrea Jones)
DES Oehme & Van Sweden

333 Andrew Duff

334 T Modest Herwig **LOC** de Groot family, Holland
DES Arend-Jan van der Horst, Holland
TEL +31 113 567 223

334 C, B Colin Walton **LOC** Cabbages and Kings, East Sussex see picture credit **136 T** for more details

335 T Garden Picture Library / Ron Sutherland
DES Anthony Paul

335 B Steven Wooster **LOC** The Erve Odinc Gardens, Holland

336 T Nicola Browne **DES** Shun Bao

336 C Jerry Harpur

336 B Ocean, Grid Teak Lounger and Cushion.
TEL 0870 24 26 28 3 **WEB** www.ocean.com

337 TR Colin Walton **DES** Walton & Flett

337 TL Jerry Harpur **LOC** Donna Karan's Roof Terrace San Francisco, CA **DES** Topher Delaney, San Francisco, CA

337 BR Garden Picture Library / Mayer/Le Scanff **LOC** Festival de Jardin de Chaumont, France

337 BL Marcus Harpur **LOC** RHS Chelsea **DES** Dan Pearson

338 Clive Streeter

339 Andrew Lawson **LOC** Denmans **DES** John Brookes

340 Jerry Harpur **DES** Topher Delaney, San Francisco, CA

341 Jerry Harpur **LOC** La Casella, Opio, France

342 T, B Malcolm Birkitt **LOC** Twickenham, Surrey
DES Andrew Wilson

343 T Clive Nichols **LOC** Charles Worthington's Minimalist Garden **DES** Stephen Woodhams

343 BR Clive Nichols **LOC** Hedens Lustgard, Sweden
DES Heidi Palmgren

343 BL Clive Nichols **DES** Paul Thompson & Trevyn McDowell

352 Elisabeth Dalton **LOC** Denmans **DES** John Brookes

ENDPAPERS Garden Picture Library / Mayer / Le Scanff